TAKE T

OUT OF PAINTING

-EXTERIORS-

Glenn Haege

America's Master Handyman ™

Edited by Kathy Stief
Illustrated by Ken Taylor
Cover and Introduction Photos
by Edward R. Noble
Back Cover Photo by Gilbert Ecks

MASTER HANDYMAN PRESS INC.

TAKE THE PAIN
OUT OF PAINTING
-EXTERIORS-

Glenn Haege
America's Master Handyman©

Edited by Kathy Stief

Published by:
  Master Handyman Press Inc.
  Post Office Box 1498
  Royal Oak, MI 48068-1498

Copyright © 1993 by Glenn Haege and Kathy Stief

First Printing 1993

Printed in the United States of America

Library of Congress Cataloging in Publication Data.

Haege, Glenn
  How to take the pain out of painting: exteriors.
  Bibliography: h.

ISBN 1- 880615-15-0

To Barbara, Eric and Heather with love.

Acknowledgments

Special thanks have to be given to the hundreds of painting professionals, retailers, wholesales, and manufacturers who have taken the time over the years to give me the information I needed to make this book possible.

People like:

Homer Formby, who would take time out of his busy schedule to show me, one on one, the best way to clean off a coating, or refinish a piece of furniture.

Don Werner, Sr. Vice President, Corporate Sales and Marketing, of the R. D. Werner Co., Inc., who gave me carte blanche to use his company's marketing and engineering materials to get you the state of the art ladder information.

Walter J. Gozdan, Technical Director of the Rohm and Haas Paint Quality Institute who opened up the resources of that great organization to me.

Gerry Grass and Pat O'Malley who gave me the foundation of my technical painting education at Sherwin Williams, and (much later), people like Ted Traskos, Chairman Emeritus of Aco.

Finally there's my three families: Barbara, Eric and Heather who provide hard work and loving support. Kathy, Kelly and Ken, the fantastic team that helps me put these books together. Brian, Maura, Lynn and all the great people at WXYT 1270, Real Talk Radio in Detroit, who make it possible for me to keep in constant contact with my ultimate information and inspiration source, my listeners.

As always, my final thanks has to go to my great listeners. Without you folks this book would not be possible.

Glenn Haege
Royal Oak, Michigan

TABLE OF CONTENTS

SUBJECT   PAGE

TABLE OF CONTENTS

SUBJECT   PAGE

TABLE OF CONTENTS

SUBJECT   PAGE

TABLE OF CONTENTS

SUBJECT   PAGE

INTRODUCTION

Glenn Haege on location for his companion book, *TAKE THE PAIN OUT OF PAINTING! -INTERIORS-*.

This book is important because:

- Painting is the quickest way to change the personality of your house.

- The fastest way to make your house express your personality.

- The most economical way to brighten and revive any home.

- The best investment you can make if you are trying to sell your house.

- A great Ego Builder. You see immediate positive results. Your house stands out. The whole neighborhood compliments you.

INTRODUCTION

Painting your home is something nice you can do for your house, your family, you, that doesn't cost a fortune. The competitiveness of the paint manufacturers has kept paint at such a bargain price it is definitely something you can afford to do.

Painting the exterior of your home makes such a difference, it is a great way to express your individuality. At the same time, paint is such a bargain that you can afford to experiment. If you don't like the result after you're done, if it no longer expresses the "real you", no big deal. Slap on another coat of paint. The house will love you for it. So will you. And you keep full bragging rights, because you did it yourself.

The paints and coatings of today are great improvements over paints available just five years ago, yet have increased very little in price. The paint manufacturers have heard your demand for quality, economy, and ease of use. They are spending vast sums in research and using advanced production techniques and huge production runs to keep prices low.

When I recommend that you pay extra for a premium paint, you can be sure that the improved quality is such that you get far more performance than you are paying for.

This book is different from most other painting books because it is laid out from the point of view of the Do-It-Yourselfer, not the paint company or the painting professional. It covers almost every problem you can have painting or staining any exterior surface.

INTRODUCTION

If you are a paint retailer, you will find that, like **TAKE THE PAIN OUT OF PAINTING! -INTERIORS-,** this book is a good training aid for your employees. It is written in simple terms and has the real world information customers need.

Most of this book is laid out on a project by project basis. I begin with a description of the project and the desired result, then take you step by step, from the prep. through the final, successful conclusion.

A majority of the paints, tools, and other products called for, are made by many different suppliers. If there are many different products that do the same thing, we will use generic terms, not product names. Whenever a product is unique, or there are only one or two products that really do the job, brand names will be used.

Now let's start painting!

Glenn Haege
America's Master Handyman

INTRODUCTION

WARNING - DISCLAIMER

This book is designed to provide general painting information for the home handyman and woman. It is sold with the understanding that the publisher and author are not engaged in rendering legal, or other professional services. If expert assistance is required, the services of competent professionals should be sought.

Every effort has been made to make this text as complete and accurate as possible, and to assure proper credit is given to various contributors and manufacturers, etc. However, there may be mistakes, both typographical and in content. Therefore, this text should be used only as a general guide and not as the ultimate source of information. Furthermore, this book contains information current only up to the date of printing.

The purpose of this book is to educate and entertain. The author and Master Handyman Press shall have neither liability nor responsibility to any person or entity with respect to any loss or damage caused directly or indirectly by the information contained in this book.

WARNING - DISCLAIMER

FOREWORD

I first met Glenn Haege more years ago than I care to remember. As one of the heads of merchandising for a large hardware chain, Glenn wasn't just interested in sales and advertising allowances, he wanted to know more about how our products worked, so he could better inform his customers. This need to inform and serve the public impressed me then, and continues to impress me now.

Over the years, Glenn and Barbara have become close personal friends of Joyce and mine. We were delighted when he went into radio full time. Glenn does a better job getting more, easy to understand, information out to more people than anyone I know.

Now, his books are making it possible to get that information to an even bigger audience. This new book, *TAKE THE PAIN OUT OF PAINTING! -EXTERIORS-* along with *TAKE THE PAIN OUT OF PAINTING! -INTERIORS-* take all the guess work out of painting and make big problems easy to solve. They are must reading for every homeowner. Joyce is sending copies to our kids. You can't get a better recommendation than that.

Homer Formby

Developer of Formby's® Furniture Care Products and author of:
WOOD and much, more.
The Complete Home Care Book.

For information on Homer Formby's book call 1-800-892-8680.

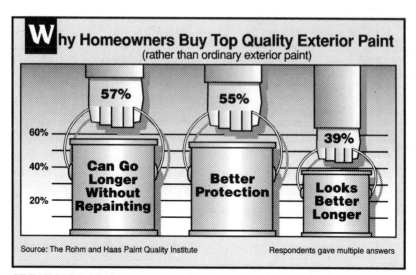

Why Homeowners Buy Top Quality Exterior Paint
(rather than ordinary exterior paint)

57%

55%

39%

60%

40%

20%

Can Go Longer Without Repainting

Better Protection

Looks Better Longer

Source: The Rohm and Haas Paint Quality Institute

Respondents gave multiple answers

GREAT EXPECTATIONS. Two out of every three homeowners said they normally purchase a top quality product when they buy exterior paint. That was a key finding in a nationwide survey of 600 homeowners conducted by the Rohm and Haas Paint Quality Institute. As the graphic above shows, most homeowners purchase top quality paint because it enables them to go longer without repainting and because top quality paint gives better protection for the home.

PAINTS & STAINS

Chapter I

**Latex? Acrylic? Oil Base?
Alkyd? Water Base? VOC?
Translucent? Penetrating?**

PAINTS & STAINS

Paint is the biggest bang for the buck in Remodeling.

A paint job is something nice you can do for your house that you don't have to budget to death. It can change your home's entire personality.

The price of equal quality paint has not increased in the past 20 years. Its value has not eroded through inflation. That makes paint a real bargain.

The reason paint is so economical is that the paint industry is highly competitive. The leading companies have chosen to use their technological improvements and production innovations to keep the price of paint down, the value up. This is a big plus for you, the consumer.

Painting is made for the Do-It-Yourselfer. Big changes can be made to your home or appearance with minimal investment in paint or tools. Paint is tough. A thin coating, barely five mils thick, is enough to protect your home's exterior from the elements.

PAINTS & STAINS

WHAT'S THE DIFFERENCE BETWEEN OIL BASE & LATEX WATER BASE PAINT?

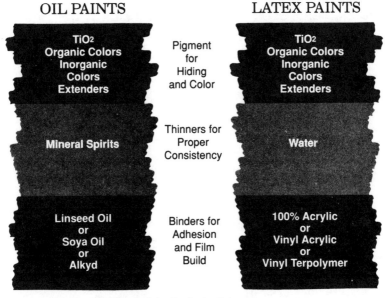

Source: The Rohm and Haas Paint Quality Institute

OIL PAINTS AND LATEX PAINTS both have three key components: pigment, thinners and binders. While similar pigments are used in both kinds of paints, oil and latex use different thinners and binders, as the chart shows.

As the Rohm and Haas chart indicates, both Oil Base and Latex Water Base Paints have the same three ingredients: Pigments, Solvents or Thinners, and Binders. Pigments give the color. Binders are the "glue" that holds the color to the surface you are painting. They are the key ingredients that give each particular type of paint its distinctive characteristics.

PAINTS & STAINS

Thinners hold the Pigments and Binders in suspension and allow you to apply them to the surface. When the paint is applied, the Thinner or Solvent evaporates, and the Pigment and Binders oxidize or "cure." This process takes anywhere from a few hours to several days.

The Pigments used in Oil Base and Latex Water Base Paints are quite often the same. The Thinners and Binders are different and give the two different paints very different performance characteristics.

In Oil Base Paints, the Linseed or Soya Oil Binders are dissolved in Mineral Spirits. As the Thinner evaporates, the Pigment and Binder form a rigid, water tight film.

PAINTS & STAINS

In Latex Water Base Paints, the chemical Binder (Acrylic, Vinyl Acrylic or Vinyl Terpolymer Polymers) are dispersed, not dissolved, in the water. When the water evaporates the Pigment and Polymer particles pack together and fuse to form a continuous, tough, but not watertight, plastic film.

CHARACTERISTICS OF
OIL BASE and WATER BASE

Oil Base Paints: are far more forgiving. They require less surface preparation, dry slower, and adhere to far dirtier, shinier, or more weathered surfaces. They can also be applied in colder weather. Oil Base Paints are designed to be worked into the surface.

Water Base Paints: dry faster, have less odor, are far more tolerant to humidity, far easier to clean up, need only soap and water, and, since they outsell Oil Base Paints better than 10 to 1, there is a greater selection of premixed colors Latex Paints lay on top of the surface.

PAINTS & STAINS

PAINTING TECHNIQUE: is very different. With Oil Base Paints you "brush in" and "stretch out" the paint. With Water Base Paints you "ladle it on" and let it "flow off" the brush. The highest quality Latex Water Base Paints include a special additive which force a heavy application.

HOW TO CHOOSE WHICH IS BEST FOR YOUR PARTICULAR PROJECT.

The decision as to which paint to use should be made on the basis of surface preparation, humidity, drying time and personal preference.

If you can't do much surface prep., and are going to paint over a rather dirty, shiny or very weathered surface, you have to choose Oil Base Paint. The water in Water Base Paint will actually combine with the grime on a dirty surface to form mud. If there's any grease, Water Base Paint will not adhere at all.

If the humidity is very high, Water Base Paint comes through like a champ. On a high humidity day, Water Base Paint will just take longer to dry. Under the same conditions, Oil Base Paint may become an ugly, sticky, never drying mess. If this happens, you may have to remove the entire paint job. Remember: it wasn't the fault of the paint, it was the fault of the painter.

If the weather is fine when you are painting, but there is a possibility of thunder storms later that day, you should know that Water Base Paint will dry and skin-coat faster to protect the job from a wash down . Oil Base Paint takes longer to dry and can be ruined by a shower.

PAINTS & STAINS

Cold effects Water Base Paint to a much greater degree than Oil Base Paints. It effects the property of the paint called "colessing" - the ability of the paint to flow together. In the cold, the chemical combination weakens and makes it so that the paint will start peeling rapidly.

When the temperature gets below 55°F, and you positively have to paint, consult your paint professional. Special purpose Cold Weather Paints are now on the market that will let you paint when the temperature is close to freezing (34°). They are expensive, but well worth the price under certain conditions.

If it's a nice day, you have a clean, well prepared surface, your choice of paints is one of personal preference. Traditionalists like Oil Base Paint's more "natural" ingredients. They like the thought of the linseed oil "feeding" and protecting the wood. Some even like the meticulous cleaning of their natural bristle brushes in turpentine or paint thinner.

One final caution: Remember, that instructions on the paint can are written for ideal conditions: 77°F temperature and 50% humidity. If it is colder, hotter, dryer, or more humid, manufacturer's instructions will have to be adapted.

Good painting conditions have a 55° to 85°F (12.5° - 29° C) temperature window of opportunity. Humidity is more forgiving. The humidity index can be anything from 0% to 80%.

PAINTS & STAINS

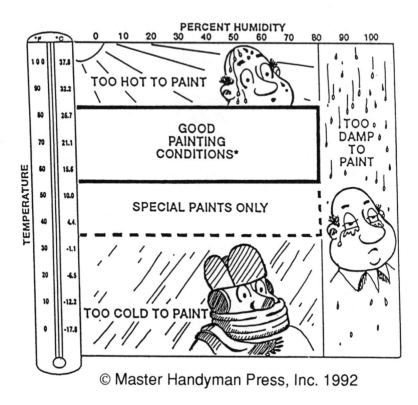

© Master Handyman Press, Inc. 1992

*The Ideal Temperature used in making most paint application specifications is 77°F, 50% Humidity. Good Painting Conditions: 55° to 85°F, 0 - 80% Humidity.

If you are outside these ranges, you may need to select special kinds of paints. In extreme ranges of heat and cold, rain or complete dryness, may not be able to paint at all.

PAINTS & STAINS

Always remember that direct sunlight is your paint's enemy. Never put paint on a hot surface It will just "boil" away.

"Boiling away" (temperature blistering) is the almost instant appearance of little tiny bubbles on the newly painted surface due to the "boiling away" of the solvent in the paint. It is caused by the application of paint on surfaces which are too hot.

Temperature blistering can also cause a condition called "chalk masking." It keeps the paint from curing properly and lets the pigment be exposed to the weather, causing excessive chalking.

If you have to paint on a hot, sunshiney day, start early in the morning and paint in the shadow.

Never paint in direct sun. The direct sun gets too hot, work behind it. Give the surface a chance to cool, before painting.

PAINTS & STAINS

Q & A
ON PAINTS
& STAINS

1. What is the most durable paint?

According to the experts at the Paint Quality Institute, the most durable exterior paint is a high quality, 100% Acrylic Latex formulation.

2. Is there a big difference between top quality and ordinary paint?

There certainly is. Generally speaking the higher the price, the better the ingredients. This translates into "the better the paint, the lower the percentage (by volume) of solvents, the higher the percentage (by volume) of paint solids.

3. What are Paint Solvents?

A paint solvent is the liquid used to hold, transport and spread paint solids. In Oil Base Paint, the solvent is usually paint thinner, mineral spirits or turpentine. In Water Base Paints, the solvent is water.

PAINTS & STAINS

Oil Base Paint solids are high in VOC (Volatile Organic Chemicals). They are what you smell when you paint with an Oil Base Paint. Since water is the solvent in Latex Paint there is little smell and very low VOC's.

4. What are Paint Solids?

Paint solids are composed of pigments and binders. Pigments give paint its color. Binders are what hold the paint together and form a firm paint film.

5. Is there a difference in Paint Pigments?

Yes! All pigments are not created equal. Generally, the same paint pigments are used in both Oil Base Paints and Latex Water Base Paints. However, the quality of the pigments varies. Generally, the more expensive the paint, the higher quality the pigment, and the more pigment is included in the paint.

As an example, both clay and Titanium Dioxide, can be used to make paint white. Clay makes paint seem nice and thick, only it tends to wash away over time. Titanium Dioxide is a lot tougher.

6. What are Binders?

Binders are the resins and other additives that hold the paint together and forms a hard surface when the paint dries. Oil Based Binders are either natural (like linseed oil) or chemical (like Alkyd). Alkyd blends consist of synthetic resins and vegetable oils.

PAINTS & STAINS

Water Based Binders are composed of Latex resin. The newest and best of these are 100% Acrylic resins.

7. What is a resin:

The resins in paint are the binders which form the film as the paint dries. These can be natural, like linseed oil, or Alkyd in the case of Oil Base Paints; or Latex or Latex Acrylic in the case of Water Base Paints.

8. What are the differences between Latex Water Base and Oil Base Paints?

Water Base Paints clean up with soap and water. They are applied thick and spread over the surface evenly. Latex paints have little odor and dry relatively fast. When dry, a Latex Paint lays on top of the wood surface and forms a tough, permeable membrane which protects the wood, but also lets it breath and expands and contracts with weather conditions.

Water Base Paint is flexible. It can be applied to damp wood with few bad effects. The paint will be thinned, but still adhere. However, if you are going to apply Water Base Paint successfully, the wood must be perfectly clean. Dust, dirt, or wood that is not in good condition will cause the paint not to adhere properly.

Oil Base Paints clean up with mineral spirits, turpentine or paint thinner. They are applied smoothly and brushed "into" the wood surface. Oil Base Paints give off a distinctive odor while drying and take at least twelve hours to dry. Oil Base Paints penetrate raw wood and form a water and air tight

PAINTS & STAINS

impermeable membrane which does not allow moisture to penetrate. However, this same characteristic does not allow wet wood to dry and stops the paint from adhering to a damp surface.

On the other hand, Oil Base Paint is far more forgiving than Water Base Paint. It can be applied over relatively dirty surfaces. Generally speaking, if you must paint a problem surface, it is better to use a high quality Oil Base Paint.

9. Does it make more sense to buy a bargain paint or a high quality paint from the perfectly practical, dollars and cents point of view?

The higher the quality paint, the easier it goes on, the longer it lasts, the less it fades, and the better it protects.

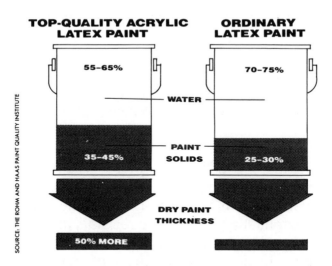

TOP-QUALITY ACRYLIC LATEX PAINT — 55–65% WATER, 35–45% PAINT SOLIDS, 50% MORE DRY PAINT THICKNESS

ORDINARY LATEX PAINT — 70–75% WATER, 25–30% PAINT SOLIDS

SOURCE: THE ROHM AND HAAS PAINT QUALITY INSTITUTE

The higher solids content of top-quality acrylic latex paints puts up to 50 percent more paint on the surface for a longer-lasting protective finish.

PAINTS & STAINS

For most of us, our home is our biggest investment. It needs all the protection we can give it. A top quality Acrylic Water Base Paint will dry to a film thickness that is about 50% thicker than an economy Water Base Paint. That means that it offers 50% more protection.

The bargain paint doesn't stay a bargain for long. It usually only lasts four or five years. Its colors will fade noticeably in the first few years.

A 100% Acrylic Latex will last ten or more years, and will retain color far more effectively.

On a straight cost comparison, the more expensive, quality paint actually works out to cost about 30 to 50% less over the life of the job.

10. What is the difference in the ingredients of paint, stain and varnish?

Knowing the primary ingredients that go into paints, stains, and varnishes, as well as the characteristics the ingredients provide, takes away the mystery.

As a general rule, the higher the Binder content, the harder and/or more reflective the surface. The higher the Solvent content, the more translucent and/or the greater its ability to be absorbed into the wood. The higher the Pigment content, the stronger and more fade resistant the color.

The chart on the next page shows the approximate difference in the percentage of Solvents, Pigments and Binders that go into paints, stains and varnishes.

PAINTS & STAINS

PAINTS, STAINS & VARNISHES

APPROXIMATE	% SOLVENT	PIGMENT	BINDER
High Gloss Trim	48	16	36
Semi Gloss Trim	46.5	25	28.5
Exterior Flat Paint	46.5	18	35.5
Exterior Flat Stain	57	29	14
Penetrating Stain	79	7	14
Satin Varnish	64.25	14.25	21.5
Gloss Varnish	68	0	32

With their high percentage of Binders, High Gloss Trim, Exterior Flat and Gloss Varnish provide the hardest surfaces. The high percentage of Solvents make it possible for penetrating stains to be drawn into the wood and penetrate. High Pigment and Solvent percentages give Exterior Flat Stain its unique ability to be "drawn" into the wood and hold its color over the years.

PAINTS & STAINS

11. How do you tell how much paint to buy?

   The amount of paint you need for a given project is determined by surface texture and by dividing the total square footage by the spread rate of the paint. Every paint is different. The average spread rate is somewhere between 250 and 500 square feet per gallon. The following chart is one adapted from The Rohm and Haas Paint Quality Institute. Don't forget trim, overhang, gutters, etc.

PAINT CALCULATION FORMULA

1. The Width X the Height of each side plus the Width X the Height from the top of the wall to the top of the peak divided by two.

2. Add to this total the Length X the Depth of all overhangs.

3. Height of each Window X the Width = Window Surface. Repeat for each Window. Add total Window Area.

4. Height of Door X Width of Door = Door Surface. Repeat for each Door. Add total Door Area.

5. Total of Lines 3 and 4.

6. Subtract the total of line 5 from the total on line 2.

7. Divide the Total of line 6 by the Spread Rate. This equals the Gallons needed for each coat of paint.

TOOLS OF THE TRADE

Chapter II

TOOLS OF THE TRADE

Basic Exterior Painting Kit

First on your list are good, professional quality brushes. Don't skimp. You'll need a 2" or 2 1/2" flat brush, a 3" or 3 1/2" brush and an angular cut trim brush if your house has a lot of French Pane Windows.

If the house has a lot of flat surfaces that have to be painted, a high quality 9" Roller, a heavy duty Roller Frame and an Extension Handle can do wonders for the speed and quality of the paint job.

As your needs, challenges and opportunities grow, so will your brush collection. Larger houses and a more varied collection of tasks, will cause you to fill out your brush collection over the years.

If you have a lot of shrubbery close to the house, inexpensive plastic drop cloths or old bed sheets will be needed to protect the landscaping. You'll need the use of a good extension ladder, preferably with stabilizers.

**The kind of coating you apply
determines the brush you should buy.**

TOOLS OF THE TRADE

COATING	TYPE OF BRUSH
OIL BASE PAINT	Natural Bristle Preferred Nylon/Polyester good.
LATEX BASE PAINT	Nylon or Nylon/Polyester
LACQUER OR VARNISH	Natural Bristle or Polyester

Never use a natural bristle brush with Latex Water Base Paint. The water in the paint and the repeated washings will ruin the bristles. Always buy professional quality brushes. The little extra cost more than pays for itself in ease of use and durability.

RULES TO LIVE BY:

NEVER USE THE SAME BRUSH FOR LATEX AND OIL BASE PAINTS.

NEVER USE THE SAME BRUSH FOR VARNISH AND ANY TYPE OF PAINT OR STAIN.

MARK BRUSHES SO YOU CAN TELL WHICH BRUSH IS FOR PAINT, WHICH FOR STAIN, WHICH FOR VARNISH.

TOOLS OF THE TRADE

2" OR 2 1/2" BRUSHES

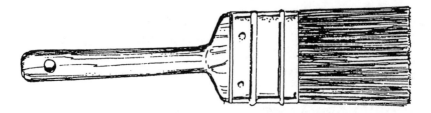

The 2" or 2 1/2" brush is the workhorse of your arsenal. It's an excellent size for many tasks: cutting in, trim work, any place where a 3" or 3 1/2" brush is too unwieldy.

I recommend a Natural Bristle brush for Varnish; a Natural Bristle or Nylon/Polyester brush for Oil Base Paint; and a Nylon, or Nylon/Polyester brush for Water Base Paint.

The average homeowner will need three 2" or 2 1/2" brushes. One for Latex, one for Oil , and one for Varnish.

Make certain that you mark each brush, so that you do not use a "Latex" brush in an Oil Base Paint. If you slip up and use a varnish brush with a pigmented coating, it should never be used with a clear coat again.

If, for some reason, you have to use an Oil Base Stain Kill, for example, and want to use Latex for the final coat, you will need two brushes. Remember that you can use interior brushes for outside work.

TOOLS OF THE TRADE

3 1/2" EXTERIOR BRUSH

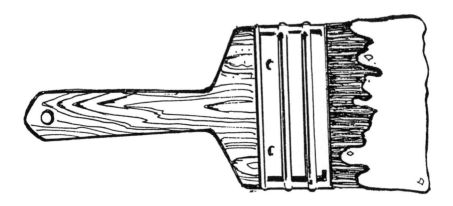

Exterior brushes are sometimes cut flat, instead of chiseled, on the theory that the paint should not be "flowed" but "ladled" onto the surface. The flat cut helps apply more paint.

If you're going to use Water Base Exterior House Paint, and most people do, buy a high quality nylon, or nylon polyester brush. A flat cut brush is best because it will help you transport and apply a lot of paint quickly. Remember, with Water Base Paint, you want to build up a 5 mil thickness. You need to apply a lot of paint.

If you're going to use Oil Base, a natural bristle brush is the best. If you like to "work in" the Oil Base Paint, buy a flat cut brush.

If you are going to apply a clear, high gloss varnish or

other coating, choose a high quality natural bristle or polyester chisel cut brush.

The same holds true for stains. If you're going to brush on a stain, make your decision according to the stain's solvent base. If a Water Base -VOC Stain, use a nylon /polyester brush. Oil Base Stains should be applied with either natural bristle, or nylon/polyester.

Don't try to be macho. 4" brushes are too big for the majority of people. They can make the job a real ordeal and don't save that much time. However, if you are Arnold Schwarzenegger, or one of the American Gladiators (I am referring to the TV personalities not an exploited underclass), grab your 4" brush and enjoy.

Those types of supremely fit individuals (you know who you are) should also use a five gallon paint pail. Put about three gallons of paint into it , grab your 4" brush and **GO!** We'll see you at the end of the house in about fifteen minutes.

1 1/2" NOTCHED (ANGULAR) SASH BRUSH

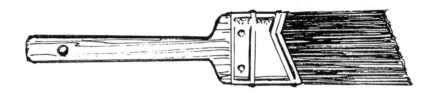

TOOLS OF THE TRADE

Especially designed for windows, Sash Brushes are about 1 1/2" to 1 3/4" wide, with a long handle that allows you to reach into the corners easily. The bristles are often cut on an angle.

RULES TO LIVE BY:

1. CHEAP BRUSHES MEAN CHEAP JOBS.

That doesn't mean you have to sell the family jewels to buy an expensive brush. If you spend $9.00 or $10.00[1] on a good 2" brush, it will never wear out. If you never loan it out, you'll never have to buy another brush.

2. YOUR BRUSH IS ONLY AS GOOD AS ITS LAST CLEANING.

If you don't clean your brush thoroughly after each use, it will get old and stiff. You'll have to buy another one.

Clean Oil Base and Varnish brushes in paint thinner or turpentine. Clean Latex brushes with soap and water. Clean and dry thoroughly, then wrap in newspaper, or store in the original container.

3. NEVER SOAK YOUR BRUSHES IN A HOT, OR CHEMICAL BRUSH CLEANER / RESTORER.

---

[1] 1992 US dollars.

TOOLS OF THE TRADE

The harsh chemicals will ruin the bristles. Train yourself to thoroughly clean your brushes after each use.

4. NEVER LET A BRUSH STAND ON ITS BRISTLES.

You are supposed to stand on your own two feet, but a brush was never meant to stand on its bristles. Brushes are very carefully designed and crafted to flow paint onto a surface. Resting the weight of a brush on its bristles for any period of time destroys their trim and shape, prevents even interior paint flow and ruins the brush.

Hang the brush by the hole in its handle, even during cleaning and drying. Store hanging, so that gravity helps the bristles retain their shape. The little extra time this takes is a very worthwhile investment.

ROLLERS

TOOLS OF THE TRADE

I recommend buying a good 9", five wire cage roller for exterior use. A five wire cage means that five, instead of four, heavy wires support the roller pad. Five wires give your roller pad better support and will keep it round longer. A good one should last for a generation or more.

ROLLER COVERS

The same thing can be said about roller covers. A $4.50 — $ 5.00[2] roller cover will give you the proper phenolic core, the proper trimmings and mixture of filaments and the nap you need to get a good paint job.

You will probably need two covers. One for Water Base, one for Oil Base Paints. You can use interior covers for exterior painting, as long as you have the right depth of pile for the job. If your walls have different textures, you will need rollers with different length nap. A smooth wall requires a roller with 3/8" or 1/4" pile or nap. A lightly textured wall requires 3/4" pile. Semi-Rough surfaces call for 1" pile. Rough surfaces require 1 1/2" pile.

Specific tasks call for specific roller pile thicknesses. We'll recommend the roller you should use, for each specific job in subsequent chapters.

When you change paints, or are painting a different texture surface that requires a different cover, splurge.

The highest quality roller cover is hand sewn lamb skin. If you are a stickler for quality, or plan to do very fine work, go

---

[2] 1992 US dollars.

for it. Properly cleaned, a good lambskin roller cover will last and last.

A good nylon-polyester roller, costs half the price and is more than adequate for most tasks.

ROLLER EXTENSION POLE

A 4' to 12' or longer wood or metal expandable pole is a necessity for painting outside. It screws into the roller handle and extends your reach and cuts hours from the job. It takes up less space and can be adjusted to just the perfect length for the job.

A Roller Extension Pole permits you to stay off the ladder. Off the ladder, with both feet solidly planted on the ground, is the safest place to be.

ROLLER TRAYS & SCREENS

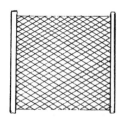

TOOLS OF THE TRADE

A heavy duty, deep well, professional model tray gives about 3/4" greater depth than standard or promotional trays. This increase in the amount of your paint supply will greatly decrease the number of trips back for refills.

An even better approach for external use is to pour a gallon of paint into the bottom of a 5 gallon pail and insert a roller screen. That way you can cover a very large area before you need a refill!

PAINTING MITS

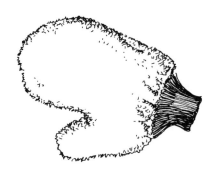

Mits are ideal for painting railings and odd sizes. They are a "must" if you have a railed deck or armed furniture. Watch out for splinters!

TOOLS OF THE TRADE

PAINT SPRAYERS

Paint Sprayers are definitely not in the basic painter's kit. Their best use is in painting furniture. Most consumer models are too weak to do a big project. Powerful HVLP (High Volume/ Low Pressure) models can do an excellent job painting or staining siding or cinder block.

Special additives have to be added to Latex Paint if it is to be used in a paint sprayer. The biggest challenge when spraying is covering too wide an area with too little paint, applying insufficient material to build up the necessary mil thickness.

If you are going to rent or buy a paint sprayer, be sure you get a HVLP (High Volume/ Low Pressure) model. An HVLP Sprayer will eliminate the many over-spraying problems and help assure that you apply the necessary mil thickness.

TOOLS OF THE TRADE

DROP CLOTHS

Canvas drop cloths are fine for professional painters. They last for years and can be washed. But they are not worth the investment for the casual D-I-Y'er. If you remodel houses for a hobby, that is a different story.

Plastic drop cloths are very good for protecting plants, shrubs, and lawn furniture. Do not use them to walk on. They are messy and become so slippery they could put you in the hospital.

Most used indoors, paper drop cloths are very good for protection of walks and other, potentially slippery areas.

A lot of people use bed sheets. They are fine for giving a little bit of protection to plants and shrubs, but do not expect them to give any really heavy duty protection.

TOOLS OF THE TRADE

STEP LADDERS

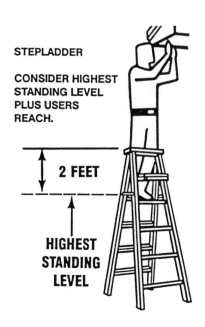

STEPLADDER

CONSIDER HIGHEST
STANDING LEVEL
PLUS USERS
REACH.

2 FEET

HIGHEST
STANDING
LEVEL

Make certain that you get a ladder that will support your weight. Many of the better ladders will have a designated weight load. Budget ladders do not have the performance characteristics you need and could cause serious injury.

You need something a little bit heavier for outside use. A wooden step ladder, or a Type I or Type II (as referred to on page 46) aluminum ladder would be ideal. You can go up to an eight foot ladder for outdoor use.

The folks at R. D. Werner and Co., Inc. , a premium ladder manufacturer, warn that you should never step higher than two feet from the top of a step ladder.[3] If you have to go higher, get another ladder.

[3] Werner Ladders, *Wood/Aluminum/Fiberglass,* 1993 edition.
For more information contact R. D. Werner Co., Inc.
Corporate Headquarters: 93 Werner Road Greenville, PA 16125-9499,
Tel: (412) 588-8600.

TOOLS OF THE TRADE

When you climb higher than two feet from the top, the ladder becomes highly unstable. It doesn't matter if you have all the neighbors, your family, the dog, cat and goldfish trying to hold the ladder steady. The only thing that succeeds in doing is putting family, friends and neighbors at risk of being squashed by a UFO (Uncontrollable Flying Object), you.

EXTENSION LADDERS

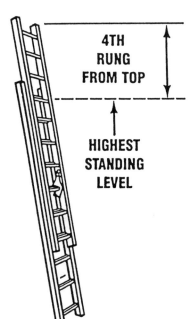

4TH
RUNG
FROM TOP

HIGHEST
STANDING
LEVEL

Good extension ladders cost money. If you're just going to use it once or twice a year, rent don't buy. If you really need an extension ladder, get a good one. I suggest a Type I or Type II.

The grade of ladder you buy is directly related to your weight. If you, plus all your tools, and the paint only add up to a total of 200 lbs., you can get away with a Type III.

If you're a big guy, like me, and the combined weight is going to be over 300 lbs., the most heavy duty ladder made(Type I A) is too light duty for you. Do what I do, **stay off the ladder!**

TOOLS OF THE TRADE

The following charts use information derived from the catalog of R. D. Werner Co., Inc. of Greenville, PA.[4] Use the first chart to help decide which class of ladder you should buy.

Rule # 1: Choose the right type of ladder for your weight.

WORKING LOAD (Combined weight of User plus Tools and Materials)	TYPE LADDER
Up to 200 Lbs.	Type III
Up to 225 Lbs.	Type II
Up to 250 Lbs.	Type I
Up to 300 Lbs.	Type IA
Over 300 Lbs.	Stay off the Ladder.

Rule # 2: Choose the right size ladder for your needs.

All of us are tempted to buy an extension ladder that is either too big, or too small. If we buy ladders by our pocket books, we buy small and "stretch our luck." Better to buy too big than too small.

---

[4] ibid.

TOOLS OF THE TRADE

CHOOSE THE RIGHT SIZE LADDER

1. MEASURE FROM GROUND TO EAVES
2. CHECK CHART BELOW FOR CORRECT SIZE

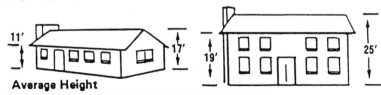

Average Height

HEIGHT TO SUPPORT POINT	BUY THIS LENGTH LADDER*	MAX. WORKING LENGTH
to 9½' Max.	16'	13'
From 9½' to 13½'	20'	17'
From 13½' to 17½'	24'	21'
From 17½' to 21½'	28'	25'
From 21½' to 25'	32'	29'
From 25' to 28'	36'	32'
From 28' to 31'	40'	35'

* This length extension ladder allows for proper overlap and a 3 ft. extension of ladder above eaves as required by minimum safety codes.

*5

Rule # 3: Set the ladder up in the proper way.

Maker certain you place your ladder up in the proper way. If it has too steep an angle, the ladder will not be steady. Make certain that your ladder base is absolutely flat (If you are on hills, etc., special levelers can be purchased that will level the ladder on an uneven terrain).

---

[5] ibid, Pg. 4

TOOLS OF THE TRADE

THE PROPER WAY TO SET UP YOUR LADDER

HEIGHT TO "V" GUTTER OR SUPPORT POINT	HORIZONTAL DISTANCE FROM SUPPORT TO "H" LADDER BASE
9½'	2½'
13½'	3½'
17½'	4½'
21½'	5½'
25'	6½'
28'	7'
31'	8'

Set ladder at proper angle by placing your toes against the bottom of the ladder. Stand erect. Extend your arms straight out. When palms of your hands contact the top of the rung, which is about eye level, the ladder is at approximately the proper angle. Check with set-up label. Use only at proper angle for better resistance to foot slip, strength of the ladder, and balance of the climber. **Support point should be at least 24"** wide at the top of the ladder in order to maintain support in the event of sideways movement.[*6]

Rule # 4: Never climb higher than the 4th. rung from the top.

Your extension ladder will become unstable if you climb higher than the 4th. rung. Hanging the paint bucket on the first or second rung is OK, but your feet **never** go there. Your weight on the upper three rungs of the ladder can make it unstable and collapse.

TOOLS OF THE TRADE

SCAFFOLDING

If you have a good sized colonial style house to paint, look into renting scaffolding. It takes a little longer to set up, and costs a little more, but you wind up saving time by being able to speed through second story work.

TOOLS OF THE TRADE

OTHER STUFF

Putty knives, scrappers, sanding blocks, sanding screens, single edged razor blades, and caulking guns, are all necessary. They are pretty well self-explanatory. If you need something special, we will explain it in detail when called for in later chapters.

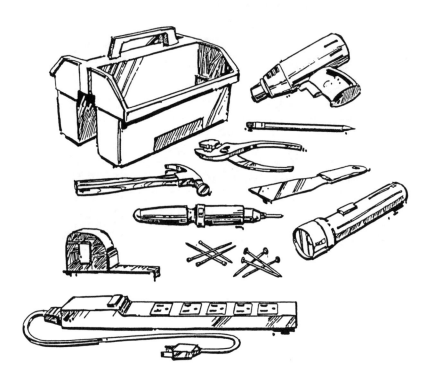

EXTERIOR PREP.

Chapter III

EXTERIOR PREP.

PROJECT: Getting ready to paint.

CONDITION: Good condition, wood sided house.

MATERIALS NEEDED: 50 Grit Sandpaper, TSP, Chlorine Bleach, Rags, Window Putty, Penetrol(TM) by the Flood Company, Caulking Compound, Water Base Stain Kill.

EQUIPMENT NEEDED: 6-8' Step Ladder, Extension Ladder (if house of 2 stories or more), Sponges, Regular Broom, Pail, Heat Gun, Putty Knife, Caulk Gun, Garden Hose with Spray Attachment, Push Broom, Goggles, Rubber Gloves, Respirator.

PROCEDURE:

1. Walk around the house and give it a good inspection. Bring a regular broom with the bristles covered with a rag along with you. Sweep away the spider webs as you go.

    If there are any hornets' nests, or bird nests, now is the time to take care of them. If there are young birds, or eggs in the nests, you may want to wait until they are flying before painting. If you can't, at least carefully remove the nests and put them in a nearby tree.

    Be on the lookout for mold and mildew. If you find mold and mildew, add chlorine bleach to the TSP solution and add a mildewcide to the first coat of paint.

EXTERIOR PREP.

2. Scrape any alligatoring, bubbling or scaling paint.[1]

3. Lightly sand using 50 Grit Sandpaper.

4. If you are going to be working on the windows, now is a good time to remove all the old, cracked putty. Soften using a heat gun and scrape away with a stiff chisel putty knife. Wipe or brush on one coat of Penetrol™ by the Flood Company. Let dry 8 hours before reglazing.

---

[1] Photos courtesy of the Rhorm and Haas Paint Quality Institute.

EXTERIOR PREP.

5. Check the caulking. If it is old, hard, and has pulled away from the corners that it is supposed to protect, replace it. Signs that caulk needs to be replaced are: pulling away from the corners and edges it is supposed to be sealing, and lack of resilience. A good test is to press the caulk hard with your thumb. If it doesn't give with the pressure, it is dried out and no longer doing its job. Soften caulk with a heat gun, or hair drier. Scrape away with a chisel or putty knife. Final clean up can be accomplished with mineral spirits.

Remember, caulking is what protects you and the rest of the family from all those drafts, and keeps the heat in and the cold out all winter long. You probably only paint the exterior of your house every 8 to 10 years. If it's been a couple of paint jobs, and the caulk is really dried out, replace it.

You will be surprised at how much caulk has improved over the past few years. There now are new, Urethane Caulks that keep their elasticity far longer.

If you are going to re-caulk using a Silicone Caulk, do the job after you paint. All other caulks should be used before painting.

EXTERIOR PREP.

6. Wash exterior surface and window frames with a 2 oz. of TSP per gallon of warm water. If there was any mold or mildew, add 2 cups of household bleach. Washing down a complete house usually takes 3 to 5 gallons of cleaning solution. Rinse off with a garden hose.

7. Let dry a minimum of 4 hours.

8. Apply a Water Base Stain Kill to the bare spots.

9. Let dry a minimum of 4 hours before painting.

EXTERIOR PREP.

PROJECT: The paint on my house is in really bad condition. I want to prepare the surface to make a "like new" foundation for my new paint job.

CONDITION: Chalking, blistering, alligatoring, checking, peeling, some rot, mold, mildew.

MATERIALS NEEDED: TSP, Chlorine Bleach, Rags, Minwax High Performance Wood Filler, Rags, Window Putty, Caulking Compound.

SPECIAL EQUIPMENT NEEDED: 6 - 8' step ladder, Extension Ladder (if 2 story or more house), sponges, regular broom, Pail, Heat Gun, Putty Knife, Caulk Gun, Garden Hose with Spray Attachment, Push Broom, Goggles, Rubber Gloves, Dual Cartridge Respirator.

TIME REQUIRED: 2 - 3 Days.

PROCEDURE:

If your home's exterior is in really bad condition, this is the time to get it fixed. Remember, preparation may take 60% or more of the time allotted to paint your house. Don't cut corners. Don't put good paint over a bad surface and blame the paint for peeling, etc.

1. Walk around the house and give it a good inspection.

EXTERIOR PREP.

Bring a regular broom with the bristles covered with a rag along with you. Sweep away the spider webs as you go.

Source: The Rohm and Haas Paint Quality Institute

EXTERIOR PREP.

If there are any hornets' nests, or bird nests, now is the time to take care of them. If there are young birds, or eggs in the nests, you may want to wait until they are flying before painting. If you can't, at least carefully remove the nests and put them in a nearby tree.

2.   Scrape and sand away any alligatoring, bubbling or scaling paint. Use 50 grit Sandpaper.

I've pictured some of the major painting problems on the next couple of pages, along with their causes and cures.

ALLIGATORING

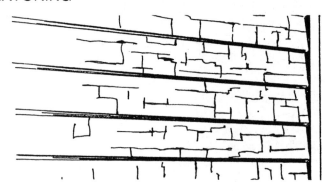

The irregular Alligatoring Pattern often happens soon after painting. If left untended, water seeps into the cracks and destroys the paint job. The cause is usually painting over a wet surface, over a not yet dry base coat, or in direct sunlight causing too rapid drying. There is only one solution, all the bad paint has got to go. Strip it off, clean thoroughly and apply a Latex Water Base Stain Kill before painting.

EXTERIOR PREP.

CHECKING

Checking is a relatively square 1/4 inch pattern. This is usually caused by too many layers of paint. If the checking is only one or two layers deep, just scrape away the loose paint and repaint. If it goes down more than three layers, it is a sign that all the old paint has to be removed. Remember, do the job right once, and you'll never have to do it again. Scrape down to bare wood, clean away all debris, even off with exterior wood filler, sand, vacuum. Paint surface with Latex Water Base Stain Kill.

BLISTERING

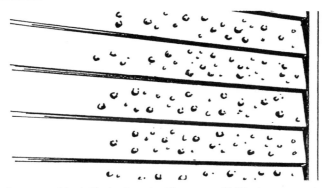

Blistering is caused by either chemical incompatibility between the new and old paints, or painting in direct sunlight on a hot day. In this case the top surface of the paint dried too rapidly and the water in the (usually) Latex Paint literally "boiled" away. To repair: scrape, then sand until smooth. Vacuum, then wash with a 2 oz. per Gallon TSP solution. After 24 hours, cover with a Latex Water Base Stain Kill.

EXTERIOR PREP.

PEELING

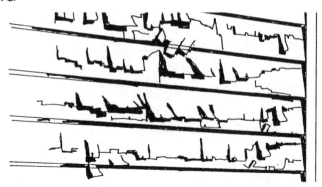

Peeling is usually a sign that the paint has been applied to wet or rotten wood or it was applied to a dirty, oily or very shiny surface. Scrape away all peeling paint, then check to see that the wood is sound. If not, repair or replace. If sound, fill depressions with Exterior Wood Filler sand smooth, and vacuum. Wash with a 2 oz. TSP per gallon of water solution, let dry then cover with a Latex Water Base Stain Kill.

3. If the paint is in bad condition, but does not yet require paint removal, you can even out the surface by filling in all the cracks and crevices with a good exterior wood filler like Minwax High Performance Wood Filler™. Do not use ordinary wood fillers. Make certain that the product you buy clearly states that it is for external use.

    External Wood Fillers are miraculous. You can shape and replace entire pieces of pillars and trim, etc. Always repair or replace, before you repaint. If a piece of siding board has rotted, you can saw the section with a key saw, then pry it out and replace.

    Before you repair or replace bad wood, do a little sleuthing. Ask yourself, "Why did the wood go wrong?" Don't just treat the symptoms. Fix the root cause before you paint or you may have to repeat the process in a year.

EXTERIOR PREP.

To smooth out the surface, fill in with Exterior Wood Filler. Smooth with a putty knife and sand.

STRIPPING:

If the surface damage is extensive, or the house has many coats of paint that are going bad, you may have to strip off the old paint to the bare wood surface. One way to remove the old paint is with a tool like the Bernz O Matic® Portable Paint Stripper.

EXTERIOR PREP.

Keep your sense of humor. This usually only has to be done once ever 30 - 50 years. That means that unless you go into the business of rehabing older houses, you will probably never have to do this job again.

WARNING: A HEAT PAINT STRIPPING TOOL IS A GREAT TIME SAVER. IT MUST BE USED WITH GREAT CARE, FOLLOWING MANUFACTURER'S INSTRUCTIONS. NEVER ALLOW A CHILD TO USE THIS EQUIPMENT. NEVER LEAVE UNATTENDED. NEVER PLACE YOUR HAND OR OBJECTS IN FRONT OF THE HEAT TUBE, OR WORK ACROSS OR DOWN WIND.

4. If you are going to be working on the windows, now is a good time to remove all the old, cracked putty. Using the heat gun, scrape away with a stiff chisel putty knife. Do not leave any residue.

5. Check the caulking. If it is old,hard, and has pulled away from the corners that it is supposed to protect, replace it. A good test is to press the caulk hard with your thumb. If it doesn't give with the pressure, it is dried out and no longer doing its job. Scrape away with your putty knife and heat gun.

6. Wash exterior surface and window frames with a 2 oz. per gallon TSP solution. If there was any mold or mildew, add 2 cups of household bleach. Washing down a complete house usually takes three to five gallons of cleaning solution. Use warm water to make the cleaning solution. Rinse off with garden hose.

EXTERIOR PREP.

EXTERIOR CLEANING SOLUTION CHART

SOILAGE	INGREDIENTS		
	WATER	TSP	BLEACH
LIGHT	2 Gals.	4 oz.	None
LIGHT WITH MILDEW	2 Gals.	4-5 oz..	4 Cups*
MODERATE	2 Gals.	6 oz.	None
HEAVY	2 Gals.	8 oz.	None
HEAVY WITH MILDEW	2 Gals.	8 oz.	4 Cups*
HEAVY WITH MILDEW & PEELING	2 Gals.	8 oz.	4 Cups*2

7. If the peeling on one or two walls is especially bad, it is a moisture problem. Go to the hardware store and get some Sure Line Vents™. Follow package installation instructions carefully.

POWER WASHING

If the surface of the house to be painted is dirty, with a disintegrating paint job, you may want to try power washing before stripping all the paint. When most of the wood and paint is still sound, a good power washing will remove most of the chaulking, loose paint, dirt, and old. At its best it will

---

2*Use Respirator in addition to rubber gloves and goggles.

EXTERIOR PREP.

leave you with a surface that needs relatively little additional scrapping and sanding before you spot prime and paint.

EXTERIOR PREP.

The down side is that you have to rent professional power washing equipment, or have the job done professionally.

I go into Power washing more extensively in my book, *FIX IT FAST & EASY!*. Here's a brief summary:

1. Soak down the lawn, flowers and shrubs around the house before power washing.

2. Cover shrubs and flowers with plastic sheets or drop clothes.

3. Use the detergent recommended by the equipment rental company. If they don't recommend a cleaner, 4 oz. dry measure of TSP per gallon of water is excellent. Add 4 cups of Household Bleach per gallon if mold and mildew are a problem.

4. Wear long sleeves and slacks, goggles and rubber gloves.

5. Power wash in the cool of the morning, never on a hot surface.

EXTERIOR PREP.

PROJECT: I have to re-putty my windows.

CONDITION: Cracked Putty, some wood rot.

MATERIALS NEEDED: Penetrol™ by the Flood Company, Window Putty, Window Points, Minwax High Performance Wood Filler™, or Red Devil One Time Wood Filler™.

SPECIAL EQUIPMENT NEEDED: Heat Gun or High Performance Hair Drier, Wire Brush.

TIME REQUIRED: 1 Day.

PROCEDURE:

1. Scrape away all old, chipped, alligatored, peeling or blistered paint from window surface.

2. Soften dry cracked putty with a heat gun. If you have to remove putty from any portion of the window, remove all of it. It is deteriorating. Do not try to patch.

   Scrape away with a large screwdriver.

3. Brush away all loose putty, wood slivers, etc.

4. Check out the wood for wood rot. If you discover a deteriorating area, scrape the bad wood out with a small chisel.

EXTERIOR PREP.

5. Refill with an exterior wood filler such as Minwax High Performance Wood Filler™ or Red Devil One Time Wood Filler™. Smooth with a putty knife.

6. Sand smooth.

7. Wipe or brush on one coat of Penetrol™ by the Flood Company on all raw wood and let stand for 8 hours before reglazing.

8. Insert new glazing points into the wood if necessary to hold in the window.

9. Reglaze with fresh putty. Putty from the can is the most economical. If time is important, consider using preformed putty ropes. The putty is all measured out, all you have to do is place it down, press it in, then smooth it into a 45° angle.

10. If you scrapped away layers of paint in some areas of the window frame, fill in and even out the surface with a product like Minwax High Performance Wood Filler™ or Red Devil One Time Wood Filler™.

11. Sand Smooth.

12. Wash with a 3 oz. per gallon TSP solution. If there were any signs of mold, mildew or dry-rot, include 2 cups of common, household, chlorine bleach.

TECHNIQUE

Chapter IV

TECHNIQUE

PROJECT: I want to paint Exterior Wood Siding with a Brush.

You can get excellent results painting a house with a brush. However, never stain a house using just a brush, the stain absorbs and dries too fast. Your job will look beautiful while you are working, but will dry blotchy.

SPECIAL EQUIPMENT NEEDED: 3-3 1/2" FLAT TIPPED BRUSH, WIDE MOUTHED 2 1/2 - 3 GAL. BUCKET.

PROCEDURE:

1. Make certain that all the paint is mixed.

2. Box paint.

3. You will work 50% faster with a large bucket that does not have to be refilled. Pour one gallon into the 2 1/2 — 3 Gal. Bucket.

4. Pour the rest of the boxed paint back into their original cans for storage.

5. Now use the brush as a carrier of the paint to the surface to be painted. Dip the brush in the paint about 1/3 of the length of the bristles into the paint bucket.

TECHNIQUE

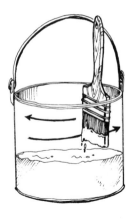

Pull the brush out of the paint and gently tap, not scrape, the brush against the sides of the paint pail.

6. Divide the surface to be painted into sections three or four boards deep by three or four feet wide.

The reason for the vagueness of dimensions is that we are all different. The area to be painted should feel natural for you and be within a comfortable work area that measures approximately one arm length and the width of your body.

When you divide the surface into imaginary sections, also consider the heat of the day, and the drying rate of paint in relationship to temperature and humidity.

TECHNIQUE

PAINTING SEQUENCE

PAINTING SEQUENCE: Always start at the top and work to the side, then down.

Keep brush strokes as fluid as possible. The faster the paint dries, the greater the potential for visibility of your start and stop strokes. Therefore the faster drying the paint, the smaller your "paint sections" should be.

7. Start from the top of the surface and work your way sideways and then down. Start in the center of a section and stroke going from the dry to the wet. Follow the grain structure of the wood.

TECHNIQUE

Transfer paint from the can to the center of the new section.

Fill in with smooth brush strokes, smoothing and filling.

TECHNIQUE

PROJECT: I want to paint my Exterior Wood, Aluminum or Vinyl Siding using the "Roller/ Brush" technique.

SPECIAL EQUIPMENT NEEDED: 3/4" or 1" Knap Roller, 5 Wire Roller Frame and Extension Handle, 3" to 3 1/2" Brush, Wide Mouthed 5 Gal. Bucket, Roller Screen.

PROCEDURE:

This is probably the quickest and best way for most of us.

1. Box the paint using steps 1 - 3 of the preceding tip.

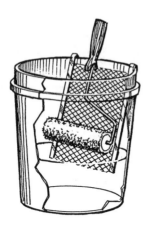

2. Pour one gallon of paint into a 5 Gallon Bucket . Hang a Roller Screen on the side of the bucket.

3. Dip the Roller with a 3/4" to 1" Knap Roller Cover into the paint. Roll excess off on roller tray, then transport the paint from the bucket to the wall surface.

4. Apply the paint with the roller to 3 or 4 board widths at a time. On Lap Siding, roll "V"s using two down, no "up" strokes.

5. Then, take a dry 3" to 3 1/2" Brush and spread the paint out over the surface. This is called "tipping" because you use the tip ends of the bristles of the brush.

TECHNIQUE

The Roller Brush Technique is a perfect job for two. The first person transports the paint to the wall with a roller.

The second person "tips in" the paint with a 3" or 3 1/2" brush.

TECHNIQUE

Use the brush to spread out the paint and "tip in" the corners and edges.

Adding the brush keeps you from putting too much pressure on the roller and spreading the paint too thinly for optimum wear.

6. Go back for another roller full of paint.

As you can see this technique was made for two people. One person transports the paint to the surface with a roller. The other "tips in" and spreads out the paint with a brush. The Roller person also starts the trim.

You will find the roller/brush technique gives you a much better, more thorough job. Use this technique even if you are a one man band on this project. You will work faster and better.

TECHNIQUE

PROJECT: I want to spray paint Exterior Wood, Vinyl or Aluminum Siding or Spray Stain Wood Siding.

MATERIALS NEEDED: Caution: Remember spraying can use up to twice the paint as the standard roller and roller/brush techniques.

SPECIAL EQUIPMENT NEEDED: Airless Paint Sprayer or HVLP (High Volume Low Pressure) Paint Sprayer.

PROCEDURE:

You can get excellent results spray painting wood, vinyl or aluminum siding. But you have to have the proper, heavy duty equipment. That means expensive. Most of us would not benefit from purchasing the quality of equipment that is necessary to get a good job.

I recommend consulting a good professional paint store that carries rental equipment and renting the equipment from them. You can also rent from a good rental equipment company.

Before you rent from anyone, make certain you understand how to operate the equipment.

If you are painting a house with a lot of windows and detail work, you want HVLP Spray equipment. If your home has a lot of broad expanses, you are better off with Airless Spray Equipment.

TECHNIQUE

IMPORTANT: CHOOSE YOUR PAINT OR STAIN FIRST, THEN MATCH THE EQUIPMENT YOU RENT TO THE PAINT OR STAIN.

Some manufacturers will suggest that their paint is not sprayable. The paint you choose is more important than the method of application. Buy the best paint for your project, then use the recommended method of application.

Many people find that the best reason for spraying, rather than Brush or Brush and Roller application is that they find it easier to apply the proper amount of paint to the surface.

Proper surface preparation is especially important when you are using spray equipment. Make certain that you follow the surface preparation instructions to the letter.

When you are sweating and swearing to yourself doing all the time consuming surface prep., keep telling yourself that the actual spraying takes almost no time at all and is a lot of fun.

CAUTION: Some paint spraying equipment uses a lot of amps of electricity to start the equipment. Make certain that your household current has the proper circuits to handle the start up of this equipment.

If you do not have access to a sufficient power supply, renting a power generator will save a great deal of aggravation running down to the basement circuit breaker box or fuse box. More important, the equipment will run cooler and more efficiently with the proper electricity.

TECHNIQUE

1. Double check to make certain that the paint says you can use it in a sprayer. Open the cans and make certain that all the paint or stain is well mixed.

2. Box the paint or stain.

3. Pour paint or stain back into original containers and re-seal that which you are not going to use immediately.

4. Check the wind. Never start spraying when it is too windy. 1 or 2 mph is OK. More than that, forget it.

5. Measure out the exact amount you will need for 100 sq. ft. and put that amount, and not a drop more or less into the paint container of your spray equipment.

6. Measure off a 100 square foot exterior section .

7. Let'er rip. Make certain that you have read the owner's manual on application technique before starting. Check to see that your equipment does not need any special additives added to the paint to enable the equipment to work without clogging.

    Here are a few application tips: Keep your spray gun pointed straight ahead, about 10" away from the surface. Use arm movements only. Never wave the spray gun from side to side with your wrist. Wrist waving will cause a very uneven paint job.

    Keep the distance of the nozzle of the spray gun a constant 10" from the surface. Accidentally pulling the spray gun back to just 18" reduces paint application drastically.

TECHNIQUE

If you wave, or pull back, coverage will look constant while the paint is wet. As it dries, the job will look splotchy and you will have to repaint.

8. Make certain that you cover the entire 100 sq. ft. section with an **even** coat of paint. Remember how long it takes you to go the distance. Don't rush. Slow, even, smooth are the watch words to success.

9. Now that you have the mind and muscle memory to guide you on how much time it takes to paint 100 square feet, fill the paint reservoir with enough paint to cover an even number of square feet, measure off the distance on the house and go for it.

You'll find that spray painting the house is fast, fun and exhilarating. Tom Sawyer could have made a million if he had let the kids in his neighborhood spray paint that picket fence.

IMPORTANT: Never stop spraying in the middle of a wall. The start and stop marks will show. If you run out of paint before finishing a wall, fill the reservoir and complete the side immediately.

Gauge yourself. If you just have a little paint in the paint reservoir, and you are about to start a new wall, stop and refill the reservoir.

You will have a natural tendency to put on too little paint. The wet hide characteristics of most paints and stains is excellent. Do not succumb to temptation. If you don't put on enough paint, you will be kicking yourself when the paint or stain dries and leaves you with a job that has to be done over again.

WINDOWS & DOORS

Chapter V

WINDOWS & DOORS

PROJECT: I want to paint brand new wood windows.

CONDITION: Beautiful, new, expensive.

MATERIALS NEEDED: Medium Grade Sandpaper, Water Based Wood Primer, Water Base Exterior Stain, or Exterior Trim Paint.

SPECIAL EQUIPMENT NEEDED: None.

TIME REQUIRED: 2 days.

PROCEDURE:

1. Lightly sand any rough areas. This is not a big job, you are just getting rid of small traces of oil and dirt, or sanding down slight rough spots.

2. Rinse off with 2 ounce TSP solution. Rinse thoroughly.

3. Decision Time. If you are going to paint the windows, apply a Latex Exterior Wood Primer (skip this step if you are going to stain the windows).

4. Wait 2 hours.

5. If you have decided to stain not paint. Apply one coat of a good Latex Exterior Wood Stain.

   If you have installed new windows in an existing house with painted siding, you'll want to paint. Use 2 coats of your preferred Water Base Exterior Trim Paint.

WINDOWS & DOORS

PROJECT: I want to put a new coat of paint on old, weathered, wood windows.

CONDITION: Weathered, Chalking, Peeling, some Wood Rot.

MATERIALS NEEDED: Putty or Exterior Wood Filler,TSP, Caulk, Oil Base Stain Kill, Latex Exterior House Paint or Exterior Latex Trim Paint.

SPECIAL EQUIPMENT NEEDED: Heat Gun, Scraper, Putty Knife and a Dry Wall Sanding Screen.

TIME NEEDED: 1-3 hours Plus, depending on number of windows.

PROCEDURE:

1. Scrape and sand wood window frames. Use a Dry Wall Sanding Screen to speed things along.

   If necessary, sand all the way down, or use a paint stripper and remove all the paint. Remember, window frames have tops, bottoms, and sides. Make certain you do a complete job. Windows are always centers of attention.

   Don't use half measures here, or the bad job will haunt you 'till next time.

2. If the surface is pitted and uneven after you have scraped all the loose paint away, smooth out the surface by filling with Exterior Spackling Compound. Sand smooth.

3. Use heat gun and large metal screwdriver to remove all old, cracked putty. If the windows are as bad as they sound, the caulk is probably in pretty bad condition also. If so, remove it all and start from scratch. Turn to the window caulking section in the Exterior Prep Chapter for some tips.

4. Wash with 4 oz. TSP solution.

5. Let dry at least 2 hours.

6. Paint with an Oil Base Stain kill such as XIM™, Kover Stain™ or Mantrose-Haeuser Hide-N Seal™.

7. Dry 4 hours.

8. Paint with 2 coats of a high quality Water Base Exterior Trim Enamel.

WINDOWS & DOORS

PROJECT: I need to repaint my Anderson™ Wood Windows.

CONDITION: Some weathering and peeling.

MATERIALS NEEDED: Putty or Exterior Wood Filler, TSP, Caulk, Oil Base Stain Kill, Latex Exterior House Paint or Exterior Latex Trim Paint.

SPECIAL EQUIPMENT NEEDED: Heat Gun, Scraper, Putty Knife.

TIME REQUIRED: 2 days.

PROCEDURE:

1. Check caulking around the frame. If hard and dry, remove caulk with a chisel point putty knife. Where needed, tap the putty knife handle with a hammer. If necessary, soften the caulk with a heat gun. Re-caulk as necessary using a Urethane style caulk.

2. Check the putty. If old and cracked, remove with a putty knife. If necessary, use a heat gun to soften the putty. Replace with new putty.

3. Scrape, then sand down peeling paint.

4. Wash with 4 oz.. TSP solution. Rinse thoroughly.

WINDOWS & DOORS

5. Let dry for 2 hours.

6. Apply 2 coats of Latex Trim Paint or Rustoleum Wood Saver™.

PROJECT: The sun has bleached my stained window panes.   I want to re-stain.

CONDITION: Sun bleached frames and sills.

MATERIALS NEEDED: TSP, Sikkens Cetol™.

SPECIAL EQUIPMENT NEEDED: None.

TIME REQUIRED: 3 days.

PROCEDURE:

1. Sand until surface powders up.

2. Wash frames and sills with a 2 ounce TSP solution. Rinse thoroughly. Dry with a cotton towel.

2. Let dry 2 hours.

3. Apply 3 coats of your choice of colors of Sikkens Cetol™. Usually you should go a little darker than the existing color. Cetol looks like varnish, but it's not. It is great for doors, too.

WINDOWS & DOORS

PROJECT: I have a 13 year old stained and varnished exterior door. I want to paint the door.

CONDITION: Yellowing, black discoloration from mold.

MATERIALS NEEDED: Coarse 80 Grit Aluminum Oxide or Garnet Sandpaper with a Hand Sanding Block, Oil Base Stain Kill, Latex Water Base Trim Paint.

SPECIAL EQUIPMENT NEEDED: Palm Sander or Sanding block. Natural Bristle Brush.

TIME REQUIRED: 2 Days.

PROCEDURE:

1. Take the door off its hinges and set it on saw horses.

2. Take all hardware off the door. Now is a great time to clean and oil the hardware. A little bit of tarnish remover might make those handles and hinges look like new.

3. Sand lightly with the coarse 80 Grit Sandpaper using a palm sander. You are not trying to sand down to the bare wood. Just make all the varnish powder. This entire task should only take about ten minutes.

4. Vacuum up the dust.

WINDOWS & DOORS

5. Wash with Liquid Sandpaper™.

6. Get all trace particles up with a Tack Rag.

7. Paint entire door, all six sides, with an Oil Base Stain Kill. Remember every door has six sides.

8. Let dry 4 hours.

9. Apply 2 coats of a Water Base Exterior Trim Paint.

Use long strokes that flow on the paint. Return the brush to the can often. Keep the bristles full of paint. Make certain that you have sufficient film build.

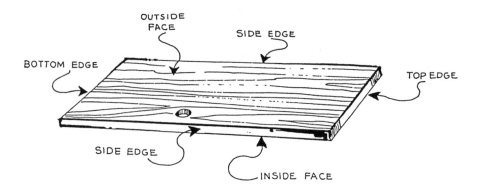

WINDOWS & DOORS

PROJECT: My oak front door has been painted many times. I want to strip it and bring it back to a natural oak finish.

CONDITION: Wood in good condition, but it has many layers of paint.

MATERIALS NEEDED: Paint & Varnish Remover, Wood Bleach, Denatured Alcohol, Minwax High Performance Exterior Wood Fill™, 80 Grit Garnet Sandpaper, Tack Rag, Stain and Urethane Varnish or Sikkens™ Exterior Door Finish.

SPECIAL EQUIPMENT NEEDED: Saw Horses.

TIME REQUIRED: 2 Days

PROCEDURE:

1. Take the door off its hinges and put on saw horses.

2. Take all hardware off door.

3. Put paint and varnish remover on door. Ladle it on as you would frost a cake. Do not paint back and forth. Apply in one direction only.

   If you desire, use Citristrip™ or Dumond Chemical removers. They will take up to 24 hours to do the job but you can pull away up to 15 layers of paint at one time.

WINDOWS & DOORS

Use twine and steel wool, or a plastic spatula to get the paint and remover out of cracks and crevices.

4. If original color, or stain, persists, wash the raw wood door with wood bleach. Then rinse with clear water to stop bleaching action.

5. Wash with denatured alcohol.

6. Inspect door. If there is wood rot, or gouges in the door, take out the bad wood and fill with an exterior wood fill like Minwax High Performance Exterior Wood Fill™. Do not use regular wood fill, it will not hold up.

7. Smooth filled areas with Sandpaper. Then sand down the rest of the door. Removing the old finish will have raised the grain of the wood. Smooth the grain with 100 Grit Garnet Sandpaper.

8. Apply stain. You can paint it on with a sponge brush or dab it on with a rag. Wipe off excess stain with a 100% cotton rag.

9. Apply 3 to 4 coat of Spar Urethane Varnish. Sand lightly with 150 Grit Sandpaper after the first coat.

If you want, you can combine the 7 th.. and 8 th.. step by using the Sikkens for Doors, a new product that combines both the stain and varnish in one coat.

WINDOWS & DOORS

PROJECT: My Old Steel Door is in really bad shape. I want to repaint and bring it back to good condition.

CONDITION: Worn, bleached paint, some rust.

MATERIALS NEEDED: Oxisolv™ Rust Remover by Solv-O Corporation, Water Base Stain Kill, Water Base Trim Enamel,

SPECIAL EQUIPMENT NEEDED: 2 1/2" Polyester Nylon Brush,

TIME REQUIRED: 2 - 3 Days

PROCEDURE:

1. Take the door off it hinges. Remove, clean, and oil hardware.

2. Spray down area that has rusted with Oxisolv™. Work it into the rust with an old paint, or better still, scrub brush.

   We are specifying a brand name here, because Oxisolv™ leaves a Zinc film behind to retard re-rusting. This is especially good for all those seam areas that have some rust.

3. Clean the door thoroughly with a 2 oz. TSP Solution.

WINDOWS & DOORS

4. Take the garden hose and rinse thoroughly.

5. Let dry in the sun until completely dry.

6. Check all the seams for breaks or tears from wear on the bottom.

7. If you see some holes or pitting, use a spot putty which you can buy at most auto supply stores. You can literally spread and smooth it with your thumb. It dries instantly.

8. Sand with a fine Sandpaper and Tack Rag as necessary.

9. Cover completely with one coat of a Water Base Stain Kill (really make certain that you get into every corner, nook and cranny. You can use a nylon polyester brush for both of the paints we are using on this project.

   Remember, all doors have six sides. Paint all of them.

10. Let dry completely. Not in the hot sun, we want the paint to dry, not fry. This is a good shade tree job. Good for the paint, good for the painter.

11. Complete with 2 coats of your favorite Latex Exterior Water Base Trim Paints. This will provide great color retention. Be sure to use enough paint. Flow it on, don't brush it off.

WINDOWS & DOORS

PROJECT: I want to paint my steel garage door.

PROCEDURE:

Apply same steps as I just described for a steel replacement door. Remember: Your garage door has six sides. Paint all of them.

If you have a lot of rust, use Oxisolv Rust Remover™ by Solv-O Corp. Then cover with a good Exterior Latex Water Based Trim Paint.

PROJECT: I want to paint my wooden garage door.

CONDITION: Good condition but very weathered.

MATERIALS NEEDED: Organic Cleaner, Water Based Stain Kill, Latex Eggshell Exterior Trim Paint.

TIME REQUIRED: 2 1/2 Days.

WINDOWS & DOORS

PROCEDURE:

Remember: a garage door, like any other door has six sides. All six sides must be prepped and painted.

1. Scrape and sand door if necessary.

2. Clean thoroughly with an Organic cleaner, such as Simple Green™, Clean Away™, Clear Magic™, or Breeze™. Rinse thoroughly.

3. Let dry a minimum of 2 hours.

4. Fill uneven areas with an Exterior Spackling Compound.

5. Sand.

6. Wipe off dust with a rag soaked in Mineral Spirits.

7. Paint door with Water Base Stain Kill.

8. Let dry one hour.

9. Apply 2 coats of a premium Eggshell Water Base Exterior Trim Paint. Apply paint with a 2 to 2 1/2" nylon polyester brush.

10. Let dry 10 hours between coats.

WINDOWS & DOORS

PROJECT: I want to paint my Fiber Glass Garage Door.

CONDITION: Good condition but the fiberglass is beginning to weather badly. I want the door to look smooth and new.

MATERIALS NEEDED: TSP, Water Base Stain Kill, Water Base Satin Exterior Trim Paint.

SPECIAL EQUIPMENT NEEDED: Elbow Grease.

TIME REQUIRED: 2 days

PROCEDURE:

1. Airborne grit and contaminants have been getting into the relatively soft skin of this door big time. We have to clean this thing really thoroughly. You'll need a scrub brush, goggles, rubber gloves, 4 oz. TSP in one gallon of warm water.

   Do a good job of scrubbing the door, really get into the pores.

2. Deluge with a garden hose or gallons of water.

3. Dry for at least four to eight hours.

4. After it is thoroughly dry, run your hand over the surface and check for chalking.

5. Apply a Water Base Stain Kill.

6. Let dry 4 hours.

7. Apply two coat of Water Base Exterior Trim Paint.

PROJECT: I want to paint my aluminum storm doors.

Don't even think of using Aluminum Paint. You will have a mess on your hands. Aluminum Paint dulls rapidly, chalks and will get all over your hands in about one month.

MATERIALS NEEDED: TSP, Water Base Stain Kill, Water Base Trim Paint.

TIME REQUIRED: 2 Days.

PROCEDURE:

KEEP THE DOG AND KIDS AWAY FROM THIS DOOR. IT WILL TAKE 7 DAYS TO CURE AFTER YOUR LAST COAT OF PAINT.

1. Clean with a solution of 3 oz. TSP (dry measure) per gallon of water.

2. Let dry thoroughly (about 2 hours).

WINDOWS & DOORS

3. Apply one coat of a Water Base Stain Kill.

4. Let dry 3 - 4 hours.

5. Apply two coats of Water Base Trim Paint in white or your choice of trim colors.

6. Remember what I said about keeping away from the door until the paint cures. Don't be fooled. The paint takes seven days to cure. Long before that the paint will feel dry to the touch, but it is not scrub resistant.

WINDOWS & DOORS

PROJECT: I want to repaint my wood storm door, storms and screens.

CONDITION: Deteriorating paint job, loose joints.

MATERIALS NEEDED: Yellow based Carpenters Glue, 50 or 80 Grit Garnet Sandpaper or Coarse Drywall Sanding Screen, Oil Base Stain Kill.

TIME REQUIRED: 1 1/2 days.

PROCEDURE:

1. Rough up the old paint surface with a coarse, 50 or 80 Grit Garnet Sandpaper, or a Sanding Screen. Don't do anything major here.

2. Wash down door or frames with a 3 oz. TSP Solution.

3. Rinse the door or frames off with the garden hose and lots of water.

4. Let dry.

5. Squeeze a Yellow Based Carpenter's Glue like Elmer's Carpenters Glue™ or Hold Tight™ Glue by Franklin, into the loose joints. Set flat until dry.

6. Paint with a Oil Based Stain Kill. Make sure you get all the nooks and crannies.

7. Let dry about 4 hours.

8. One or two coats of finish coat of your choice. Again, be sure to get into all the nooks and crannies again.

   This should be a fast job. Storms and screens are very thin stock, it is difficult to keep paint on.

PROJECT: I want to paint my aluminum storms and screens.

CONDITION: If Raw Aluminum: Don't Paint. Brighten with Metal Gleam™, then seal with All Shield™.

CONDITION: If Pre-Painted at Factory follow these directions.

MATERIALS NEEDED: TSP, Water Base Stain Kill, Water Base Exterior Trim Paint

SPECIAL EQUIPMENT NEEDED: None.

TIME REQUIRED: 2 Days.

PROCEDURE:

1. Wash down with 3 or 4 oz. TSP Solution.

2. Rinse with garden hose.

3. Let dry thoroughly.

4. Apply one coat of Latex Water Base Stain Kill.

5. Let dry 3 to 4 hours.

6. Apply two coats of Water Base Exterior Trim Paint.

PROJECT: I want to revarnish wooden sliding glass door wall frames.

CONDITION: Varnished, good but yellowed.

MATERIALS NEEDED: 80 and 120 Grit Sandpaper, Varnish Remover, TSP, Household Chlorine Bleach, Stain of your choice, V.O.C. Type Spar Varnish.

SPECIAL EQUIPMENT NEEDED: None.

TIME REQUIRED: Depending on Condition.

PROCEDURE:

1. Sand thoroughly. If you can not get all the yellowed varnish off using Sandpaper, remove chemically with a varnish remover.

WINDOWS & DOORS

2. Repair and replace any rotted or gouged areas. Shape and sand.

3. If any wood is discolored, use a Chlorine Bleach full strength. Wipe it on until the wood lightens, then stop the chemical action by rinsing with clear water.

4. Wash with a 4 oz. TSP solution.

5. Rinse thoroughly.

6. Let dry for 2 or 3 hours.

7. Apply one coat of Stain if desired.

8. Let dry.

9. Apply 2 or 3 coats of V.O.C. style Finish.

PROJECT: I want to paint over the varnish on wooden sliding glass door wall frames.

CONDITION: Varnished, good but yellowed.

MATERIALS NEEDED: TSP, 50 & 100 Grit Garnet Sandpaper, Minwax High Performance Exterior Wood Filler™, Liquid Sandpaper, Oil Base Stain Kill, Oil Base Exterior Wood Trim.

SPECIAL EQUIPMENT NEEDED: None.

WINDOWS & DOORS

TIME REQUIRED: Depending on Condition.

PROCEDURE:

1. Rough up the surface with the 50 Grit, then smooth out the surface with the 100 Grit Garnet Sandpaper.

   Remember all doors have six sides. Ideally, you would have taken the doors off their tracks to work on them. If this is not possible, at least treat the side edges with the rest of the door.

2. Gouge out any deteriorated wood areas, then fill with Minwax High Performance Wood Fill™ or similar product (it must say for exterior use on the label). Smooth out and sand as necessary.

3. Wash off with a 3 - 4 oz. TSP Solution. Add 2 cups of common Household Chlorine Bleach to every gallon of water if there is a mold and mildew problem.   Rinse thoroughly with clear water.

4. Let dry 4 hours.

5. Wipe on Liquid Sandpaper™.

6. Wait 30 minutes.

7. Apply a coat of an Oil Base Stain Kill.

8. Let dry 4 hours.

9. Apply 2 coats of Oil Base Exterior Trim Paint.

WINDOWS & DOORS

PROJECT: I want to recondition and paint wooden sliding glass door wall frames.

CONDITION: Painted.

MATERIALS NEEDED: TSP, Latex Water Based Stain Kill, Latex or Oil Base Finish Paint.

SPECIAL EQUIPMENT NEEDED: None.

TIME REQUIRED: 2 days.

PROCEDURE:

1. Scrape and Sand as needed.

2. Repair and replace any rotted or gouged areas. Shape and sand.

3. Wash with a solution of 4 oz. (dry measure) of TSP per gallon of water.

4. Rinse copiously.

5. Let dry 4 hours.

6. Apply one coat of Latex Water Based Stain Kill.

7. Apply two coats of your favorite Oil or Water Base Exterior Satin Enamel Trim Paint.

WINDOWS & DOORS

PROJECT: I want to paint metal sliding glass door wall frames.

CONDITION: Good.

MATERIALS NEEDED: TSP, 100 Grit Sandpaper, Water Base Stain Kill, Oil or Water Base Exterior Enamel.

SPECIAL EQUIPMENT NEEDED: None.

TIME REQUIRED: 3 Days

PROCEDURE:

1. Scrape and sand as needed.

2. Wash down with 4 oz. TSP solution.

3. Let dry a minimum of 4 hours.

4. Apply one coat of Water Base Stain Kill.

5. Let dry 4 hours.

6. Apply 2 coats of your favorite Oil or Water Base Exterior Enamel.

WOOD FRAME SIDING

Chapter VI

WOOD FRAME SIDING

PROJECT: I have a brand new house and want to paint it.

CONDITION: Brand new.

Seriously consider whether you want your house to be painted, or whether stain will do. While paint is the conventional treatment for a new house, stain will do just as good a job of protecting the surface.

Stain resists bubbling and flaking. It soaks into the wood and, compared to paint, it adds less "mil build" or coating thickness that will have to be sanded and scraped off later.

My advice is to go to the paint store and look at samples of wood that have been stained. If you like the stained look, go with it. Your first two or three "paint jobs" can actually be stain. You can always paint later.

PROJECT: Stain Job.

MATERIALS NEEDED: TSP, Water or Oil Base Stain.

Oil Based Stain soaks into the wood surface more. Water Base Base Stain lays on top of the surface. Many traditionalists like Oil Base Stain's absorption quality. In addition to being easier to apply and clean up, the new Water Based Stains have Acrylic Resins that resist fading.

WOOD FRAME SIDING

SPECIAL EQUIPMENT NEEDED: Extension handle for Roller, Extension Ladder, Ladder Stabilizers.

TIME REQUIRED: 2-3 Days.

PROCEDURE:

1. Inspect exterior for rough edges. Sand and caulk as needed.

WOOD FRAME SIDING

2. Wash entire exterior with a 3 oz. TSP solution. You'll need at least 3 or 4 gallons for an entire house. This is a great 2 person project. Apply TSP solution with a push broom. Let wait a few minutes, then rinse off liberally with a garden hose.

3. Let dry overnight.

4. Box the stain. That means pour the individual cans of stain back and forth between the stain can and an empty pail. Then, when each can is mixed, mix all the stain you plan to use on the job in one large 5 gallon container.

   Once the stains have all been mixed to a uniform color, pour all but one can back into their original containers and seal.

5. Stain may be applied by either the spray, brush and roller, or brush method. Stain goes on so fast that any way you choose is OK.

   Read the label directions carefully. Do not stretch the stain beyond the recommended square footage.

   Always work behind the sun. Stain is mostly solvent and a little pigment. It will "boil off" easily under the glare of a hot summer sun.

WARNING: Never stop, even for coffee, in the middle of a wall. Do a complete wall, or you will be able to see where you stopped work for years.

WOOD FRAME SIDING

PROJECT: Paint Job.

CONDITION: Brand new.

MATERIALS NEEDED: TSP, Sandpaper, Caulk, Water Base or Oil Based Primer, Water Base or Oil Based Exterior House Paint, Water Base or Oil Based Trim Paint (if desired).

Whether you choose an Oil Base or Water Base Primer, or House Paint is entirely up to you. Here are some considerations: Oil Based Primers soak into the wood. Water Base Water Based Primers stay on top of the surface. Both are thin coatings and let the house "breath" and dry properly.

A Water Base Paint expands and contracts. It "breathes" and lets moisture pass through the coating. When thoroughly cured, an Oil Base Paint forms a tough, air tight, water tight shell, that neither expands nor contracts. It provides maximum protection, but can be made to blister, by the heat of the sun drawing the moisture through the wood.

Confused? Over 90% of all exterior paint sold is Water Base Paint.

SPECIAL EQUIPMENT NEEDED: Roller Extension Handle, HVLP Spray Gun (if desired), Extension Ladder, Stabilizers.

TIME REQUIRED: 3 1/2 days.

WOOD FRAME SIDING

PROCEDURE:

1. Inspect exterior for rough edges. Sand and caulk as needed.

2. Wash entire exterior with a 3 oz. TSP solution. You'll need at least 3 or 4 gallons for an entire house. Apply with a push broom. Let wait a few minutes, then rinse off liberally with a garden hose.

3. Let dry overnight.

4. Apply one coat of primer. You can tint the primer towards your final coat.

5. Let dry 3 to 4 hours. That probably means that you can start your final coat as soon as you have worked your way around the house.

6. You are now ready for your two finish coats of paint. Box the paint.

   That means, pour the paint back and forth between two paint pails that are slightly larger than the original can. Be sure you scrape all the residue from the origininal can into the mix.

WOOD FRAME SIDING

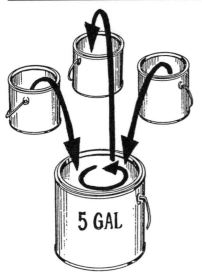

5 GAL

After the paint is completely mixed, make certain that the color is uniform by pouring all the paint you plan to use for an entire coat, in one large 5 gallon container and mixing.

Then, pour the paint back into the original storage pails until needed. If necessary, a mildewcide can be added to the final coat.

You can use either a roller and brush combination or an HVLP paint sprayer. If you are going to spray, rent an HVLP paint sprayer. Don't waste your time with the inexpensive DIY models. You won't get a large enough coverage area, or put on the necessary mil finish.

I prefer applying the paint with roller and brush because you get the feel of the paint and can teach yourself to apply the proper mil finish.

Wind speed is your enemy. Never spray against the wind. If the wind starts picking up (over 10 m.p.h.), do yourself a favor and **STOP.**

7. Let dry overnight.

8. Make certain that the paint is perfectly dry before applying a second coat of paint.

WOOD FRAME SIDING

PROJECT: I want to paint weathered exterior wood siding.

CONDITION: Poor condition. Peeling, chalking, black spotting mold and mildew.

MATERIALS NEEDED: Bleach, TSP, Non Clay Based Wood Filler such as Red Devil One Time ™, or Perm-E-Lastic™; Water Base Stain Kill, Premium Water Base Exterior Paint, Mildewcide additive.

SPECIAL EQUIPMENT NEEDED: Heat Gun for stripping bad areas, Sander.

TIME REQUIRED: 2 1/2 - 5 days.

PROCEDURE:

The peeling problem was probably caused by bad surface preparation the last time the house was painted, or by spreading the paint too thin. Both are very common problems.

Paints, especially Water Base Paints are never made to be spread thin. When spread thin, they do not have the proper resilience to flex during wide seasonal temperature swings and can flake off.

Black splotching is usually caused by mold and mildew. To test, dip a cotton swab into pure bleach and hold it against a blackened spot for 60 seconds. If the black

WOOD FRAME SIDING

is gone when you remove the swab, the problem is mold and/or mildew. If the black is still there, the problem is dirt. Ninety-five percent of the time, the problem is mold and mildew.

1. Scrape all the loose paint off. If the house is 50—60 years old, severe blistering or peeling may have taken place. If the peeling goes all the way down to the raw wood, you will have to remove the paint from the entire surface.

   Check Paint Removal in the Exterior Prep Chapter. Sand, use a heat gun, or one of the new heat strippers to loosen paint. Scrape away old paint.

   Most of us will never have to do this to our homes. Left to natural weathering, you would need at least five to ten paint jobs, before paint removal becomes essential. Assuming a life expectancy of seven to twelve years, that means a house should only need paint removal, once every 35 to 120 years.

2. If the paint does not have to be removed, scrape and brush off the loose paint, then fill the scraped area 8 feet in height or lower with exterior (non clay based) wood filler and sand smooth. You now have a perfectly smooth painting surface as far up as the eye can see.

3. Wash the entire surface to be painted with a solution of 4 oz. TSP to a gallon of water. You can spray on the solution with a garden sprayer, then scrub with a long handled push broom. Rinse off with a Garden Hose.

   WARNING: TSP solution is going to be splattering all over the place. Be sure you are wearing goggles, long sleeved shirt, pants, and cuffed rubber gloves.

WOOD FRAME SIDING

If mildew is a problem, add 2 cups of bleach per gallon.

Soak all shrubs, flowers and grass with water before spraying a bleach/TSP solution. Put drop clothes over delicate plants.

4. Let dry for a minimum of 4 hours. If you are working your way around the house, this should not cause any inconvenience.

5. The next step is to spot prime the bare spots with a Water Based Stain Kill. You can tint the stain kill to match your final paint if desired.

6. Let dry 2 or 3 hours.

7. Check for chalking with your bare hand. If chalking is present, add Emulsa Bond™ by the Flood Company to the first coat of paint.

8. Apply two coats of premium exterior Water Base House Paint. Let dry overnight between coats. If mold or mildew is a problem, add a mildewcide to the final coat of paint.

WOOD FRAME SIDING

KEEP YOUR COOL!

FOR THE BEST PAINT JOB

START
IN
THE
SHADE.

START
WEST SIDE
IN THE AM

Make certain you always paint in the shade and follow the sun. During the summer, the temperature of siding in the direct sun will often go

FINISH
EAST SIDE
IN THE PM

up to 120° F. This effectively boils off the solvent and can cause rapid chemical changes to occur to the pigment and filler, ruining the job.

END IN
THE
SHADE.

WOOD FRAME SIDING

PROJECT: The Paint is peeling from my wood frame garage. I want to repaint with something that lasts.

You'd think that garages and the rest of the house are the same thing. They are not. The wood on garages have a great deal more stress than the accompanying house. The reason for this is that garages are unheated, uncooled and uninsulated.

Since they never dry out, the sun is constantly trying to leach the moisture out of the damp wood, through the paint. This often causes flaking on the sides of the garage which have the greatest exposure to the sun. Installing Shurline ™ Vents will save the new paint job.

CONDITION: The garage is in good condition. However, the paint job is badly weathered. The southern exposure is peeling badly.

MATERIALS NEEDED: TSP, Shurline™ Vents, Water Base Stain Kill, Premium Water Base House Paint.

SPECIAL EQUIPMENT NEEDED: 3/4" Drill.

TIME REQUIRED: 2 - 2 1/2 Days

PROCEDURE:

1. Scrape and sand thoroughly.

WOOD FRAME SIDING

2. Use exterior wood filler to fill noticeable holes in surface due to blistering and peeling.

3. Sand smooth.

4. Drill 3/4" holes on southern exposure and install Shurline™ Vents. This is a very simple job. Follow instructions on package.

5. Wash entire garage with a solution of 4 oz. (dry measure) TSP. Rinse with garden hose.

6. Apply a coat of Water Base Stain Kill to all exposed wood.

7. Let dry 3 - 4 hours.

8. Check for chalking with your bare hand. If chalking has occurred, add Emulsa Bond™ by the Flood Company to the first coat of paint only.

9. Apply 2 coats of a premium Water Base Water Base House Paint.

10. Let dry 24 hours between coats.

WOOD FRAME SIDING

PROJECT: I have a wood and cinder block garage. The paint on both the wood and the cinder block is peeling badly. I want to solve the problem.

CONDITION: Peeling of block and wood surfaces, some black spotting.

MATERIALS NEEDED: Round Wood Breather Vents for wood surface, Chlorine Bleach, TSP, Water Base Stain Kill, Water Base Paint.

SPECIAL EQUIPMENT NEEDED: Roller with Extension Handle, Garden Sprayer.

TIME REQUIRED: 2 1/2 days.

PROCEDURE:

1. Scrape and brush surface of both block and wood surfaces.

2. Drill holes and put in round Shurline™ Wood Breather Vents.

3. Test black spots with a bundle of cotton swabs dipped in pure household Chlorine Bleach. If black spots disappear, they are mold and mildew.

4. Combine one pound of TSP to 5 gallons of water. If cotton swab test was positive, add one gallon of Chlorine Bleach. Wash down wood and cement blocks.

WOOD FRAME SIDING

Wear goggles, cuffed rubber gloves, long sleeved shirt, slacks and shoes.

Spray on solution with a garden sprayer. Keep wet for a few minutes, then scrub with a long handled push broom.

5. Rinse with a garden hose.

6. Let dry for 2 or 3 days.

7. Cover bare spots with a Water Base Stain Kill.

8. Let dry for 4 hours.

9. Check for chalking with your bare hand. If present, add Emulsa Bond to the first coat of paint only.

10. Ask your retailer for a full bodied Acrylic Water Base Paint. Apply two coats.

11. Wait at least one day between coats.

WOOD FRAME SIDING

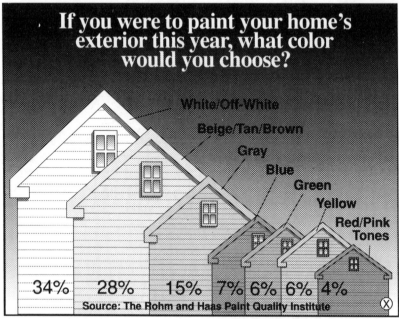

If you were to paint your home's exterior this year, what color would you choose?

White/Off-White
Beige/Tan/Brown
Gray
Blue
Green
Yellow
Red/Pink Tones

34% 28% 15% 7% 6% 6% 4%

Source: The Rohm and Haas Paint Quality Institute

COLOR IT NEUTRAL. What color would most homeowners like to paint their home's exterior? According to a nationwide survey, almost two out of three would choose some variation of white, beige or brown. The next most popular color was gray. The survey was conducted by the Rohm and Haas Paint Quality Institute, which interviewed a total of 600 homeowners in six U.S. cities: Boston, Chicago, Dallas, Ft. Myers, Los Angeles and Portland, Oregon.

T1-11 & OTHER SIDINGS

Chapter VII

T1-11 & OTHER SIDING

T 1-11 is a manufactured product. It may look like ordinary wood, but it isn't. It is really a collection of wood fibers, going every which way. It therefore has no defined grain pattern.

This means that you can not do anything to bring out the grain, there isn't any. Since T 1-11 is just a collection of wood fibers, it does not have uniform absorbency.

When working with T 1-11 you should follow two rules:

1. Use a Water Base Stain or Paint, not an Oil Base Stain or a Paint.

2. The coating must be one that will stay on top and keep a solid look for a long time.

Now that we've discussed what T 1-11 is, let's get to the project at hand.

PROJECT: I want to stain new T1-11.

CONDITION: Beautiful and new.

MATERIALS NEEDED: TSP, Water Base Exterior Stain.

**SPECIAL EQUIPMENT NEEDED:
Extension Handle for Roller or HVLP Paint Sprayer, Extension Ladder (if needed) and Ladder Stabilizers.**

T1-11 & OTHER SIDING

TIME REQUIRED: 2 1/2 Days

PROCEDURE:

1. Wash T 1-11 with a solution of 2 or 3 oz. (dry measure) TSP to a gallon of water. Use a long handled push broom to scrub it down. Rinse off thoroughly with a garden hose.

2. Let dry 2 to 3 hours.

3. Pour all the stain you are going to use, in a common five gallon pail. Boxing the stain makes certain it is uniform. There are many good Latex Exterior Stains. The best and longest lasting will be Latex Acrylic Water Born Stains.

4. Be sure to follow the stain manufacturer's recommendations for the spread rate of the stain. Each manufacturer will give you a specific spread rate based on surface texture: Rough or Smooth. Follow these rules to the letter.

Do not attempt to stretch. These products wet hide, so they look like they are covering completely when wet. But they can dry blotchy and you will have to go back and restain the entire surface.

If you do not have a lot of windows, you can spray. If you are going to spray, make certain that you use a professional quality HVLP (High Volume/Low Pressure) sprayer.

If you have a few windows apply stain with a roller.

T1-11 & OTHER SIDING

Rolling is just about as fast as spraying. The Roller Cover should have a 3/4" nap so that it can get into all the cracks and crevasses. Be sure and use a long extension handle on the roller. That way you can eliminate most of the ladder work.

Insects love T 1-11 and Shingles. If you want you can add an anti-bug additive, and/or a mildewcide.

Once you start staining, do not stop, even for a glass of water, until an entire side has been completed. If you stop mid wall, you will be able to see the overlapped area when the stain dries. One coat is all you need.

PROJECT: I want to paint weathered, already stained, T 1-11 Siding. Can I restain, or do I have to paint?

CONDITION: Some wood rot, flaking, mold, mildew.

MATERIALS NEEDED: TSP, Exterior wood filler, such as Minwax High Performance Wood Filler™, Mildewcide, Water Base Exterior Wood Stain.

SPECIAL EQUIPMENT NEEDED: Extension Handle for Roller, Extension Ladder and Ladder Stabilizers.

TIME REQUIRED: 2 1/2 Days.

T1-11 & OTHER SIDING

PROCEDURE:

Stick with the stain. Once you start using paint, there is no turning back. As a general rule, T 1-11 looks better, longer with a stain.

1. Chip out any dry rot. If there are wood pecker drilling holes, etc.. Fill holes with exterior wood filler. Minwax High Performance™ is the most expensive, but worth the extra price.

2. Wash exterior with a solution of 3 oz. TSP (dry measure) to a gallon of water. Add 2 cups of bleach per gallon to clear mold and mildew from siding.

3. Follow same instructions as for new T 1-11. Start with Step #3.

If you decide that you have to paint, paint. I recommend two coats of a premium Latex Water Base Exterior House Paint.

T1-11 & OTHER SIDING

PROJECT: I've got a dark colored plywood shed. I want to paint it a light yellow.

CONDITION: Good condition. Some flaking and mildew.

MATERIALS NEEDED: TSP, Minwax High Performance Wood Filler™, Water Base Stain Kill, Latex Flat or Satin Exterior House Paint, Mildew Additive.

SPECIAL EQUIPMENT NEEDED: Roller with Extension Handle.

TIME REQUIRED: 2 Days.

PROCEDURE:

1. Prep as you would any wooden exterior. Begin by checking for dry rot. Chisel out dry rot area and fill in with a good exterior wood filler. Minwax High Performance Wood Filler™ is very good for this.

2. Sand filled in areas, then sweep away spider webs around the structure.

3. Wash with a solution of 3 oz. TSP (dry measure) solution. If there is a little mildew problem, add 4 cups of household chlorine bleach to the mix. Rinse thoroughly with a garden hose.

4. Let dry 4 hours.

T1-11 & OTHER SIDING

5. Cover bare spots with a Water Base Stain Kill like 1-2-3 Bin™ or Kilz II™. One gallon will cover about 300 square feet. You can use roller with this.

6. Repaint the entire area with a Water Base Flat or Satin Exterior House Paint. If mildew is a problem, add a Mildewcide, such as Sta-Klean™ to the final coat of paint.

7. Follow instructions on can for drying time between coats.

PROJECT: I want to stain my new Cedar Siding.

CONDITION: Brand new.

MATERIALS NEEDED: TSP, your choice of an Oil Base Semi Transparent Stain or a Latex Stain, Mildewcide.

SPECIAL EQUIPMENT NEEDED: Extension Handles for Roller and Brush, Tank Sprayer.

TIME REQUIRED: 1 1/2 Days.

PROCEDURE:

1. Wash down the Cedar Siding with a light 2 oz. per gallon TSP and water solution to get rid of any accidental dirt or grease that may have gotten onto the siding during construction.

T1-11 & OTHER SIDING

Spray on solution with a tank sprayer in 8' sections. Brush lightly with a push broom. Rinse off with a garden hose. Be sure to wear goggles.

2. Let dry overnight.

3. Stain with your choice of an Oil Base Semi-Transparent Stain or a Water Base Exterior Stain. The Oil Base Stain will allow the grain structure to show through. The Water Base Stain will mask the wood grain, but let the texture show through.

Apply with a long handled roller-3" brush combination. Special Extension Handles for the Paint Brushes are also available.

PROJECT: I want to stain my weathered Cedar Siding.

CONDITION: Good but weathered with some mildew.

MATERIALS NEEDED: TSP, Chlorine Household Bleach, your choice of an Oil Base Semi-Transparent Stain or a Water Base Latex Exterior Stain, Mildewcide.

SPECIAL EQUIPMENT NEEDED: None.

TIME REQUIRED: 1 1/2 Days

T1-11 & OTHER SIDING

PROCEDURE:

1. Brush away spider webs,etc., from exterior with a broom. While you are doing this inspect siding condition for dry rot, mildew, etc.

2. Prep as you would any wooden exterior. Begin by checking for dry rot. Chisel out dry rot area and fill in with a good exterior wood filler. Minwax High Performance™ is very good for this.

3. Sand filled in areas, then sweep away spider webs around the structure.

4. Wash with a 3 oz. TSP solution. If there is a little mildew problem, add 2 cups of household Chlorine Bleach per gallon to the mix. Rinse thoroughly with a garden hose.

   Be sure to wear goggles.

   If you prefer, you may power wash Cedar Siding. No TSP or Chlorine Bleach will be needed if you do this.

5. Let dry overnight.

6. Stain siding with your choice of an Oil Base Semi-Transparent Stain or a Water Base Exterior Stain. If mildew was a problem, add a mildewcide. If bugs have been a problem, add an anti bug additive.

   The stain may be applied by sprayer or by a roller/ brush combination.

T1-11 & OTHER SIDING

Make sure that you do not spread stain farther than recommended by the manufacturer.

ALTERNATIVE: If you want you may use a water seal or a sealer/toner such as those made by Olympic, Cabot Penofin or Thompsons instead of the stain. The good ones contain a UV Blocker, but none will hold the color very long.

PROJECT: I want to stain the new exterior Redwood Siding on my house.

CONDITION: Brand new.

MATERIALS NEEDED: Laundry Detergent or Organic Cleaner, Oil Base Semi Transparent Exterior Stain.

SPECIAL EQUIPMENT NEEDED: Extension handle for roller.

TIME REQUIRED: 1 1/2 Days.

PROCEDURE:

1. Clean the surface lightly with laundry detergent or Organic Cleaners such as Simple Green™, Breeze™, Clean Away™ or Clear Magic. Do not use TSP on Redwood. This is just a light cleaning to get rid of any grease or dirt that may have gotten on the wood during construction.

T1-11 & OTHER SIDING

You can spray on the detergent with a garden sprayer, then use a long handled push broom for this. Rinse off with a garden hose.

2. Let dry 4 hours.

3. Apply one coat of a Semi Transparent Oil Base Exterior Stain. If you want, look into some of the specialized products by Penofin™ or Sikkens™ by Akzo™.

A roller-3" brush combination is best for the initial stain application. Make certain that you do not exceed the recommended square footage while applying the stain.

Never stop in the middle of a wall. Always continue staining until you get to the end of a wall or the overlapping will show.

PROJECT: I want to restain my weathered Redwood Siding.

CONDITION: Weathered.

MATERIALS NEEDED: Laundry Detergent or Organic Cleaner, Semi Transparent Oil Base Exterior Stain.

SPECIAL EQUIPMENT NEEDED: Extension Handle for roller, Garden Sprayer.

T1-11 & OTHER SIDING

TIME REQUIRED: 1 1/2 Days.

PROCEDURE:

1. Brush off all spider webs, etc. with a broom.

2. Power wash with clear water or wash down the siding with laundry detergent or an Organic Cleaner.

   Do not use TSP on Redwood.

   If there is mildew on the siding, you can add 2 cups of Household Bleach per gallon of water to the spray. Spray on cleaner with a garden sprayer, one eight foot section at a time. Brush in soapy mixture thoroughly with a long handled push broom, then rinse off with a garden hose.

   Be sure to wear goggles.

   If the siding is severely weathered, or grayed, power washing is preferred.

3. Let dry overnight.

4. Go to Step #3 of the directions for staining new Redwood Siding.

LOG & WOOD SHINGLES

Chapter VIII

LOG & WOOD SHINGLES

PROJECT: I want to stain my new log house.

CONDITION: New Cedar Logs.

MATERIALS NEEDED: Water Base Exterior Stain, Mildewcide, Anti Bug Additive if needed.

SPECIAL EQUIPMENT NEEDED: Professional quality airless spraying equipment.

TIME REQUIRED: 1 1/2 Days

PROCEDURE:

Use same procedure as for staining wood sided house. The only difference is that you are better off applying the stain with professional quality airless spraying equipment.

Add Mildewcide and/or Anti Bug Additive if needed.

If you rent this equipment, check to see that you have sufficient electric power to run the equipment properly. Start up draws a lot of amps and may cause problems with the circuit breakers. You may want to rent a portable generator for this project and give the spray equipment all the power it needs.

LOG & WOOD SHINGLES

PROJECT: I want to restain my log house. When finished, I want the discoloration to be gone and the wood logs to look like they did 10 years ago.

CONDITION: Severely weathered. Discolored from Ultra Violet Rays, turning black at bottom from mold and mildew, some dry rot, but basically very sound.

MATERIALS NEEDED: Chlorine Bleach, TSP, Deck Brightener, Mildewcide, Acrylic Stain, Perseverance (large economy size).

SPECIAL EQUIPMENT NEEDED: HVLP Paint Sprayer or Roller with long extension handle. Dual Canister Respirator.

TIME REQUIRED: 4 - 6 Days.

PROCEDURE:

1. First thing to do is check out the black discoloration along the bottom of the siding. Dip 3 or 4 cotton swabs in pure household Chlorine Bleach. Press the bundle of Cotton Swabs against the black for 30 seconds. If, when you remove the cotton swabs, the black is gone, it's the creeping curd, otherwise known as mold. If it's not gone, it's just plain old fashioned dirt.

2. Soak down surrounding plants, lawns, flowers, shrubs, etc. before you do Step #3.

LOG & WOOD SHINGLES

IF IT'S THE CREEPING CRUD:

3. Wash walls down with a mixture of 4 oz. TSP, 1 Gallon of Chlorine Bleach, 2 Gallons of warm water. If you want to power wash the house instead, just brush on a solution of 1 gallon of Bleach to 2 Gallons of Water, before you power wash with clear water. The Bleach will kill the mold and mildew. The power washing will clean off all the accumulated stains.

IMPORTANT: Soak surrounding lawns, bushes, flowers, shrubs, before the Bleach and water or Bleach and TSP treatments.

WARNING: Which ever you choose, wear goggles, cuffed rubber gloves, dual canister respirator, long sleeved shirt and slacks. A high concentration of Chlorine Bleach can be very hard on the lungs.

IF THE COTTON SWAB TEST PROVED IT IS NOT THE CREEPING CRUD:

4. Wash down the siding with a good Deck Brightener.

   Soak surrounding lawns, bushes, flowers, shrubs, before the Bleach and water or Bleach and TSP treatments.

BACK TO REGULAR DIRECTIONS:

5. Rinse thoroughly with a garden hose.

6. Let dry for one day.

7. Re-stain with a Acrylic Solid Color Stain. Make certain that you do not cover more space than recommended by the manufacturer.

PROJECT: I want to varnish my new log house.

I no longer recommend varnishing a large exterior structure such as a house or cabin. There are new, better products on the market. The look will be the same, or better. The protection will be far greater.

CONDITION: New Cedar or Pressure Treated Logs.

MATERIALS NEEDED: Chlorine Bleach, TSP, Deck Brightener, Mildewcide, Sikkens CETOL 1 and CETOL 23 Plus.

SPECIAL EQUIPMENT NEEDED: Powerwashing Equipment, Garden Sprayer.

TIME REQUIRED: A lot.

PROCEDURE:

1. The wood has to be really dry, so the first thing is to apply a coat of non-film-building wood preservative and

just let the cabin sit for at least six months. In the Northern parts of the US that probably means not doing any more until next year.

2. Use a Garden Sprayer to spray on a solution of 4 oz. TSP plus 1 quart or Household Bleach to 3 quarts of water.

3. Let the solution stay on the wood for 15 minutes. Keep it wet while the solution is working. In practice, this means that the size of the area you should clean at any one time is restricted by how much you can keep wet. In practice, that means that you should only clean one side or less of the cabin at a time.

4. Power wash the area with clear water. Set the power washer for no more than 1500 psi.

5. If blue fungi or rust stains remain, treat the specific areas with a solution of 4 oz. of Oxalic Acid Crystals to one gallon of warm water. Let sit for 15-20 minutes, then power wash off with clear water.

WARNING: Oxalic Acid is dangerous stuff. Make sure you are wearing boots, slacks, long sleeved shirt and goggles. A respirator would not be a bad idea. Keep pets, kids, spouse and rubber necking neighbors away from the danger area.

6. Let dry 2 good dry days.

7. Re-chink if necessary.

LOG & WOOD SHINGLES

Green or Pressure Treated Logs: (Over 18% moisture content when built)

8. Apply 3 coats of Cetol 1, a minimum of 24 hours apart. Apply with a long haired, natural bristle brush.

9. Wait 2 years.

10. Apply one coat of Cetol 23 PLUS.

11. Apply another coat of Cetol 23 PLUS every 3 to 4 years.

Kiln Dried or Air Dried Logs (18% of lower moisture content when built).

8. Apply 2 coats of Cetol 1, a minimum of 24 hours apart. Apply with a long haired, natural bristle brush.

9. Wait 24 Hours.

10. Apply one coat of Cetol 23 PLUS.

11. Apply another coat of Cetol 23 PLUS every 3 to 4 years.

This is a long tedious process, but the results are outstanding.

LOG & WOOD SHINGLES

PROJECT: I want to revarnish my Cedar Log Cabin. When finished, I want the discoloration to be gone and the logs look like they did 10 years ago.

As stated above, I no longer recommend varnishing a large exterior structure such as a house or cabin. There are new, better products on the market. The look will be the same, or better. The protection will be far greater.

CONDITION: Severely weathered. Discolored from Ultra Violet Rays, turning black at bottom from mold and mildew, some dry rot, but basically very sound.

MATERIALS NEEDED: CITRISTRIP™ by Specialty Environmental Technologies, Inc., Chlorine Bleach, TSP, Deck Brightener, Mildewcide, Sikkens CETOL 1 and CETOL 23 Plus.

SPECIAL EQUIPMENT NEEDED: Powerwashing Equipment, Garden Sprayer.

TIME REQUIRED: A lot.

PROCEDURE:

1. According to the Sikkens' people, the first step must be to remove the old varnish. This can be a long, time-consumming practice. Basically there are three ways of doing this: Chemical, Sanding, Water Blasting.

LOG & WOOD SHINGLES

Sanding takes too long. Water Blasting has to be done by professionals. Chemical can be done by any Do-It-Yourselfer.

STRIPPING PROCEDURE:

a. Apply Non-Wax Based Stripper liberally. I recommend CITRISTRIP™ for this job because it is a very environmentally friendly MNP based stripper. It is also very thick, and will stay wet up to 48 hours, so you can do the entire cabin at one time.

   Apply liberally with a brush. Stroke in one direction only, like you were frosting a cake. You are going to use a lot of stripper. Ask your paint store professional to help you estimate the quantity that you will need.

b. The stripper works in just 20 to 30 minutes, so you should be able to start removing it right away. I recommend having a cold pop or some ice tea before re-starting.

c. Put on your goggles. Powerwash with clear water. Use the low pressure setting (about 1500 psi water pressure).

d. Let dry.

e. Inspect to see that varnish has been stripped.

f . Repeat where necessary. If you are going to continue working, do not let the surface dry, go directly to the next step. If you break for the night here, hose down the wood with a garden hose before the next step.

2. Use a Garden Sprayer to spray on a solution of 4 oz.

LOG & WOOD SHINGLES

TSP plus 1 quart or Household Bleach to 3 quarts of water.

3. Let the solution stay on the wood for 15 minutes. Keep it wet while the solution is working. In practice, this means that the size of the area you should clean at any one time is restricted by how much you can keep wet. In practice, that means that you should only clean one side or less of the cabin at a time.

4. Power wash the area with clear water. Set the power washer for no more than 1500 psi.

5. If blue fungi or rust stains remain, treat the specific areas with a solution of 4 oz. of Oxalic Acid Crystals to one gallon of warm water. Let sit for 15-20 minutes, then power wash off with clear water.

WARNING: This is dangerous stuff. Wear goggles, long sleeves, slacks, and boots. Keep kids, pets, and all rubberneckers away.

6. Let dry 2 good dry days.

7. Re-chink if necessary.

8. Apply 3 coats of Cetol 1, a minimum of 24 hours apart. Apply with a long haired, natural bristle brush.

9. Wait 24 hours.

10. Apply one coat of Cetol 23 PLUS.

11. Apply another coat of Cetol 23 PLUS every 3 to 4 years.

LOG & WOOD SHINGLES

PROJECT: I want to stain my new cedar shingled house.

CONDITION: Brand New Wood Shingles.

MATERIALS NEEDED: Water Base Exterior Stain, Mildewcide, Anti Bug Additive if needed.

SPECIAL EQUIPMENT NEEDED: Professional quality airless spray equipment.

TIME REQUIRED: 1 1/2 Days

PROCEDURE:

1. Use same procedure as for staining new wood sided house. The only difference is that you are better off applying the stain with professional quality airless spray equipment.

If you rent this equipment, check to see that you have sufficient electric power to run the equipment properly. Start up draws a lot of amps and may cause problems with the circuit breakers. You may want to rent a portable generator for this project and give the spray equipment all the power it needs.

LOG & WOOD SHINGLES

PROJECT: I want to re-stain my cedar shingled house.

CONDITION: Good but weathered.

MATERIALS NEEDED: TSP, Chlorine Household Bleach, Water Base Exterior Stain, Mildewcide, Anti Bug Additive if needed.

SPECIAL EQUIPMENT NEEDED: Professional quality airless spray equipment.

TIME REQUIRED: 1 1/2 Days

PROCEDURE:

Follow the instructions for Weathered Cedar Siding, above, except that siding must be hand washed. Power washing is not recommended for wood shingles. The high pressure water could rip off the shingles.

If you rent professional quality airless spray equipment, check to see that you have sufficient electric power to run the equipment properly. Start up draws a lot of amps and may cause problems with the circuit breakers. You may want to rent a portable generator for this project and give the spray equipment all the power it needs.

NON WOOD SIDINGS

Chapter IX

NON WOOD SIDINGS

PROJECT: My Aluminum Sided House was supposed to stay looking good forever. Boy does it need a paint job.

You are a lot luckier than you think. Aluminum Siding Is one of the best surfaces in the world on which to paint. Good preparation is very important. It will take two thirds of the time if you do it right.

CONDITION: Severely worn. Can almost see the bare aluminum in some spots. Some mold and mildew in shaded area. A great deal of re-caulking needed.

MATERIALS NEEDED: Acrylic Latex Water Base Paint, Mildewcide, Anti Chalking Additive.

SPECIAL EQUIPMENT NEEDED: Extension Ladder with Stabilizers or Scaffolding, Paint Sprayer or Roller with Extension Handle.

TIME REQUIRED: 4 days.

PROCEDURE:

1. Cleaning is extremely important. Your best bet is to have the Siding Power Washed. You may rent the equipment or hire professionals to do this. Do not try using those little water pressure power sprayers. They do not have the power to do this job. A heavy duty power unit that creates water pressure of at least 2,000 p.s.i. is needed.

NON WOOD SIDINGS

I have included a short Powerwashing section in the Exterior Prep. section of the book. There is a far more extensive description in my book, *FIX IT FAST & EASY!*

If you want to save money, you can wash the surface down with a solution of 4 oz. TSP, 1 Gallon Bleach, and 2 Gallons water. A minimum of at least 10 gallons for the average size house.

Clean a 6 to 8 foot wide section of the house at a time. Spray on TSP solution with a garden sprayer. Keep it moist for at least 2 or 3 minutes. Brush vigorously with a push broom. Rinse with a garden hose. If any soiling remains, you'll have to get up on a ladder and work away with a garden hose.

2. Let dry at least 24 hours. While you are waiting, carefully inspect the caulking around the house. If it has drawn away from corners, or is no longer resilient, remove the old caulk and recaulk. You can soften caulk with a heat gun, or hair drier. Scrape off with a putty knife. Final clean up can be accomplished with mineral spirits.

3. Apply a full bodied, top of the line Acrylic Latex Water Base Exterior Paint. This can be either applied by hand with a brush/roller technique, or sprayed on. For most people the brush/roller technique is easier.

If you want to spray, you will need to get a special additive, Flotrol™ by the Flood Co., to enable this very thick paint to be shot through the nozzle. Do not try to just add water. You will ruin the paint.

NON WOOD SIDINGS

You should also rent one of the new HVLP spray guns. Old fashioned guns and light weight D.I.Y. units can not get sufficient product on the surface to do the job.

The three most common mistakes with spray painting are 1: Applying too thin a coat of paint; 2: Waving the paint gun instead of spraying straight ahead; 3: Applying too thick a coat of paint. If your application is too thin, you will have to redo the job. If you wave, the result will be blotchy, and you will have to redo the job. If you over apply, you may use up to twice the paint necessary.

The coverage rate for Acrylic Latex Water Base Paint is 400 square feet to a gallon. To test to make certain that you are applying paint at the proper rate, measure off a ten by ten foot section (100 square feet). Put one quart of paint on that section. Once you get the flow going you can just keep repeating the process.

With a good spray job you can put on enough paint so that you only need one coat. However, remember, spraying often uses double the paint that brush or brush and roller techniques use. This means that you can use the same amount of paint with a one coat spray job and a two coat brush or brush and roller job.

If you brush and roll, you will need two coats.

If you are going to re-caulk using a Silicone Caulk. Do the job after you paint. All other caulks should be used before painting.

NON WOOD SIDINGS

PROJECT: I want to paint the aluminum siding on my aluminum sided motor home.

CONDITION: Good, but travel worn. A little dinged up.

MATERIALS NEEDED: Dirtex® or Organic Cleaner, Imron® Polyurethane Primer and Enamel.

SPECIAL EQUIPMENT NEEDED: HVLP Spray System or Roller with Extension Handle.

The reason that I am giving different specifications for the aluminum siding on your motor home than the aluminum siding on your house, is that you do not drive your house over dirt roads at fifty miles an hour.

The brand I am specifying is a Catalyzed Polyurethane finish. It is the only product of this caliber that has yet been released for use by the D.I.Y.'er. Imron® coatings by the DuPont Company are so tough they paint bridges with them. They are also tough to use.

The manufacturer recommends that the primer be applied to a thickness of 10 mils wet/ 5 mils dry. I have been preaching for ten years, trying to get D.I.Y.'ers to apply paint to a 5 mil thickness. Most of you are still putting it on at a 2 to 3 mil thickness. I'm recommending a product that should go on at a 10 mil spread rate.

NON WOOD SIDINGS

Before you try it, ask yourself if you have the mental attributes to pour on a paint that costs like liquid gold, at a thickness of two to five times what you normally paint. If the answer is no, ask the professional paint dealer for the name of a professional who will do the painting for you.

TIME REQUIRED: 4 days.

PROCEDURE:

1. Clean the exterior of the motor home or trailer thoroughly with your choice of Dirtex® or an organic cleaner. I like Dirtex for this because the ammonia will do a good job of cutting through all that road gunk that may have accumulated over the years. Important: Make certain that you never use Chlorine Bleach with any ammonia based product. Ammonia and Chlorine make a poison gas.

2. Mask everything you do not want painted. Everything. Use lots of newspaper cut to size, and various thicknesses of masking tape. This should be an art form. I've allocated 2 days of the entire 4 day process to this job. If you get paint on something that you don't want painted, it will take a jack hammer to get it off.

3. Roll or spray on the Imron® primer. This coating must be 10 mils thick when wet. I prefer the HVLP (High Volume, Low Pressure) Spray System.

4. Let dry 4 to 6 hours.

5. Apply Imron® gloss coat. This finish should be applied to a thickness of 5 mils. Dupont makes Imron available in a very broad range of colors.

NON WOOD SIDINGS

PROJECT: I want to paint the Vinyl Siding on my house. I want to change color and bring back the "sheen" the siding had before it got old and dull looking.

CONDITION: Rough, dull looking. The outer surface "sheen" has been worn away from years of wear and tear by the elements.

PROCEDURE: Follow Aluminum Siding Re-Painting Instructions.

NON WOOD SIDINGS

PROJECT: I want to paint new exterior face brick.

CONDITION: It's in good condition, but I want to make it look like something I saw in a design magazine.

PROCEDURE:

1. Don't do it.

2. Please don't do it. You'll regret it. Your brick was made to look natural and weather gracefully.

3. OK, you've been warned. If you really must do this, you can use Exterior Latex Paint. But you would probably be better off, shooting pictures of your home's exterior, then taking the pictures to the best professional and industrial coatings store in your community.

Show them the pictures, and the magazine article, or what-ever, that has given you this great idea. Let them make recommendations. It may well be that you want to call in a professional on this, or at least, use a high tech coating. Let the professionals tell you the best they can do and how much it will cost. Learn and listen. It is still not too late to back out of this project.

NON WOOD SIDINGS

PROJECT: I want to paint a weathered brick surface.

CONDITION: Old and weathered.

MATERIALS NEEDED: 20° Muratic Acid, Water Base Stain Kill, Water Base Exterior Latex Paint.

SPECIAL EQUIPMENT NEEDED: Power Washing Equipment, Spraying Equipment.

TIME REQUIRED: 3 to 5 days.

PROCEDURE:

1. Power wash the entire surface. An alternative to this would be to give the brick surface a Muratic Acid Bath. I suggest that you use professionals for both of these alternatives. If you must do the job yourself, opt for the power wash. Use the same directions as for power washing vinyl or aluminum siding in the Exterior Prep Chapter.

2. Let dry one or two days.

3. Cover entire surface with an Water Base Stain Kill.

4. Let dry 4 hours.

5. Cover with 2 coats of a premium Water Base Exterior House Paint.

NON WOOD SIDINGS

ALTERNATIVE PAINTING PROCEDURE:

If you want to use a professional on this, take pictures to an industrial painting supply store. Ask about some of the high tech industrial coatings. What you use, depends upon what they have in your neck of the woods. There are some very good, super strength coatings, available. However, they have to be applied professionally. Some of them even require that the equipment operator be wearing an air tank.

PROJECT: The Brick on the lower portion of my colonial has been severely discolored by the chalking of aluminum siding. I want to paint the brick.

Don't paint, stain. You'll get much better, more long lasting results.

CONDITION: Worn brick with chalking.

MATERIALS NEEDED: Cement Stain.

SPECIAL EQUIPMENT NEEDED: Power Washing equipment; Spray Gun or Roller with long Extension Handle.

TIME REQUIRED: 4 Days.

PROCEDURE:

1. Power wash the entire brick surface. I recommend that

NON WOOD SIDINGS

this be done by a professional. He may suggest that the entire house, including the Aluminum Siding be done. This may be a good idea. If you don't like the looks of your aluminum siding after it has been power washed, turn to the aluminum siding painting instructions at the beginning of this chapter.

When you select the power washing service, I suggest that you choose some organization that has a good track record power washing professional buildings. Take a look at a few of their jobs and make certain that you are happy with the results.

2. Let stand 48 dry hours.

3. Mask Aluminum Siding.

4. Spray or roll the Cement Stain in your choice of colors on Brick.

PROJECT: The face brick from my house was splattered with paint from repainting the down spouts year ago. I want to remove the splatters and make the brick look uniform.

CONDITION: Good condition but weathered and paint splattered.

NON WOOD SIDINGS

MATERIALS NEEDED: Heavy Bodied Paint & Varnish Remover like CITRISTRIP™, Safe & Easy #2, OR ZIP STRIP II, Silicone Water Repellent.

SPECIAL EQUIPMENT NEEDED: Power Washing Equipment.

TIME REQUIRED: Up to 1 Week.
(Don't worry, most of this is just drying time.)

PROCEDURE:

1. Put a Heavy Bond Paint & Varnish Remover on the paint splatters.

2. Wait at least 45 minutes.

3. Power wash the entire homes brick surface, including the paint splattered areas. It is best to use a professional power washing company for this job. Best to look for one that does a lot of commercial work. They are used to working with brick.

4. Let dry for 48 dry hours.

5. Spray on a coat of Silicone Water Repellent to seal the brick. It is much better to rent a good spray gun for this large job, rather than try to roll it on, or use a small light duty spray gun.

NON WOOD SIDINGS

PROJECT: I want to paint a new cement, cement block or Adobe house.

CONDITION: New

Don't paint, stain. You'll get much better, more long lasting results.

MATERIALS NEEDED: TSP (if dirty), Cement Stain.

SPECIAL EQUIPMENT NEEDED: Power Washing Equipment (if dirty), Airless Paint Spray Equipment or Roller with 3/4" Knap Roller Cover and Long Extension Handle.

TIME REQUIRED: 2 1/2 - 5 days.

PROCEDURE:

1. Power wash the entire cement surface.

2. Let stand 48 dry hours.

3. Mask Windows.

4. Spray or roll the Cement Stain in your choice of colors on Brick.

NON WOOD SIDINGS

PROJECT: No dice. I want the look of paint, not stain, on my new cement, cement block or Adobe house.

CONDITION: New

MATERIALS NEEDED: TSP (if dirty), Water Base Exterior Paint.

SPECIAL EQUIPMENT NEEDED: Power Washing Equipment (if dirty), Airless Paint Spray Equipment or Roller with 3/4" Knap Roller Cover and Long Extension Handle.

TIME REQUIRED: 2 1/2 - 5 days.

PROCEDURE:

1. Power wash the entire cement surface.

2. Let stand 48 dry hours.

3. Mask Windows.

4. Box Paint.

5. Paint with 2 coats of a Water Base Latex House Paint. Use either Airless Spray Painting Equipment or a Long Handled Roller with 3/4 to 1" Knap and a 2 1/2 - 3 Gallon Bucket. The Roller/Bucket method goes very fast. Be prepared to use a lot of paint.

NON WOOD SIDINGS

PROJECT: I want to repaint my cement or cement block house.

CONDITION: Paint is weathered and flaking badly. A lot of the paint has come off.

MATERIALS NEEDED: TSP, Water Base Stain Kill, Water Base House Paint.

SPECIAL EQUIPMENT NEEDED: None.

TIME REQUIRED: 2 1/2 - 5 days.

PROCEDURE:

Cement block is damp on the inside. It absorbs humidity from the house. Natural heating of the cement block exterior by the sun, draws the moisture through the block and out through the paint.

Along the way, the moisture picks up soluble salts from the cement. Soluble salts destroy paint.

1. Scrape and brush all the loose paint off the block. Do a real good job at this. If necessary, use a wire brush, or a sanding wheel brush attachment to your portable drill. Use goggles. If you use a sanding wheel, you should also wear a respirator.

2. Scrub down with a solution of 4 oz. TSP per gallon of water. If there is mold and/or mildew, add 2 cups liquid Chlorine Bleach to the solution and wear a respirator.

NON WOOD SIDINGS

Use a scrub brush for this. Wear rubber gloves. Rinse off with a garden hose. Use lots of water.

3. Let dry at least 4 hours.

4. Paint entire block surface with a Water Base Stain Kill. If you had a mold or mildew problem, add a mildewcide.

5. Let dry 4 hours.

6. Paint with 2 coats of a Water Base House Paint.

PROJECT: I want to repaint my Gunite or Adobe Sided House.

CONDITION: Paint is weathered and flaking badly. A lot of the paint has come off.

MATERIALS NEEDED: TSP, Water Base Stain Kill, Water Base House Paint.

SPECIAL EQUIPMENT NEEDED: Power Washing equipment; Spray Gun or Roller with long Extension Handle.

NON WOOD SIDINGS

TIME REQUIRED: 4 Days.

PROCEDURE:

1. Power wash the entire surface. I recommend that this be done by a professional. When you select the power washing service, I suggest that you choose some organization that has a good track record power washing professional buildings. Take a look at a few of their jobs and make certain that you are happy with the results.

2. Let stand 48 dry hours.

3. Mask windows, etc.

4. Spray paint the entire surface with a Water Base Stain Kill. If you had a mold or mildew problem, add a mildewcide.

    I recommend spray painting over rolling for Gunite because of the irregular surface. If you have a rather smooth adobe sided house, you will get equally good results with a Roller and Long Extension Handle. Use a 3/4" Knap Roller Cover and a 2 1/2 to 3 Gal. Bucket.

5. Let dry 4 hours.

6. Spray 2 coats of a Water Base House Paint.

NON WOOD SIDINGS

PROJECT: Latex Paint crumbling off of Asbestos shingles. Painted two years ago. Want to repaint.

CONDITION: Shingles in good condition, but paint crumbling off shingles.

MATERIALS NEEDED: Caulking compound, Oil Base Exterior Stain Kill, Emulsibond by Flood, Premium Exterior Water Base House Paint, Water Base Exterior Trim Paint.

SPECIAL EQUIPMENT NEEDED: Power washing equipment.

TIME REQUIRED:

PROCEDURE:

1. Inspect shingle surface carefully. Make certain that it is the paint not the shingle that is the problem. Shingle siding should last for fifty-sixty years.

WARNING: If Asbestos shingles are not in good condition, they have to be discarded. This does not mean simply dumping them into the trash. This is a serious pollution problem. Call your City Hall and get instructions.

NON WOOD SIDINGS

The usual procedure is to double bag, document, and personally take them out to a hazardous waste dump where they have to be identified and stored in a specially dedicated area. Please do not try to sneak by here. We only have one planet and we're trying to keep it safe for our grand kids.

2. If shingles are sound, power wash all crumbling paint off surface. If the pocket book permits, you are usually time and energy ahead using a professional for this part of the job. If not, or if you have a mad desire to do every part of the process yourself, rent power washing equipment. You need a generator rig for this, not one of the little power washing sprays you see advertised.

3. Caulk as needed.

4. Apply a Water Base Exterior Stain Kill, such as KILZ Total One, X-I-M® X-Seal, Kover Stain™ orUltra Hide™ Stain Kill can be sprayed, rolled or painted on with a brush. If the surface is very chalky, add Emulsibond™ by the Flood Company, to the Stain Kill.

5. Let dry three or four hours.

6. Apply a premium Exterior Water Base Paint. This paint may be sprayed, rolled, or painted on with a brush. You must be very careful not to spread paint on too thinly. Water Base Paint should never be applied at more than 350 to 400 square feet per gallon.

NON WOOD SIDINGS

CAUTION: Unless you are very proficient at using a paint sprayer, you would probably be best off using a combination of roller and paint brush. The most common problem in using a sprayer is applying paint too thinly. Also, a special additive must be used when using Water Base Paint in a paint sprayer. Ask your paint store for instructions and cross check with the manual for your paint sprayer.

TECHNIQUE: Using a roller and brush combination is a great 2 person job. One person uses the roller on an extension handle to transport the paint to the surface and apply rough coverage.

The second person follows with a 3 or 3 1/2" brush and "fills in." That way all the little cracks and crevices that you find with shingles get filled in beautifully, and the person with the brush doesn't even need a paint can. If this sounds confusing, read the Brush/Roller instructions in the "Technique" chapter at the beginning of the book.

OPPORTUNITY: If flying or crawling insects have been a problem around your house (they love to make their home around nice, loose shingles), add an insecticide, such as Enviro-Chem's CPF 2 D™ additive to the last coat of paint. It will work wonders.

7. Check windows, gutters, trim, etc. for chalking. If chalking has started to occur, add Emulsa-Bond™ by the Flood Company to the finish coat.

MISCELLANEOUS

Chapter X

MISCELLANEOUS

PROJECT: I want to paint my new Picket (or Rail) Wood Fence.

I suggest that you use stain, not paint.

CONDITION: New.

MATERIALS NEEDED: TSP, Acrylic Exterior Wood Stain.

SPECIAL EQUIPMENT NEEDED: Paint Sprayer or Long Handled 9" Roller.

TIME REQUIRED: 4 Days.

PROCEDURE:

1. Wash down fence with a 2 oz. TSP solution, or a 10 to 1 Organic Cleaner solution. Rinse with garden hose.

2. Let dry for 2 days.

3. Spray or roll on one coat of Acrylic Exterior Wood Stain in your favorite color.

   One coat of stain is fine. However, if you were to choose to paint, you would need two coats of Oil Base or Latex Water Base Exterior House Paint, or Semi Gloss Latex Water Base Exterior. If you choose to paint, get a premium Acrylic Water Base Paint.

MISCELLANEOUS

If you choose Latex (and I heartily recommend it), make certain that you do not spread the paint to thin. Keep to the recommended spread rates. Also, if you are spraying, you will need to buy Floetrol™, an additive made by the Flood Company, to add to the paint you are spraying or it will clog the sprayer.

PROJECT: I want to re-paint my 3 to 5 year old painted wooden fence.

CONDITION: Severe paint break down, flaking, chipping, wind abrasion, some mold and wood rot.

MATERIALS NEEDED: TSP, Household Chlorine Bleach, High Performance Wood Filler, Acrylic Water Base Stain Kill, Exterior Water Base Flat House Paint.

SPECIAL EQUIPMENT NEEDED: Paint Spray Gun or Roller with Extension Handle.

TIME REQUIRED: 4 days.

PROCEDURE:

1. Inspect the fence carefully. Pull the weeds around the fence so you can get a really good look at it.

2. Scrape and brush away as much of the flaking as possible.

3. Make up a cleaning solution of 2 gallons warm water, 1 gallon bleach and 2 oz. or TSP. Spray on solution with a garden sprayer. Do an 8 foot section at a time. Keep the wood moist for a couple of minutes, then brush vigorously with an Acid Brush.

    This is a cuffed rubber gloves, goggles and dual canister respirator project. If it is hard on you, it will be hard on the plant life too. Remember to soak down all the grass, flowers, shrubs and trees with water before you start with the Bleach/TSP mixture.

    Rinse with Garden Hose.

4. Let dry for two dry days. Average temperature should be at least 60°F.

5. Replace any wood that has rotted through. Gouge out dry rot areas and fill with High Performance Wood Filler or Mr. Max Wood Fix™.

    Sand smooth.

6. Apply one coat of Acrylic Water Base Stain Kill. Wait 4 hours.

7. Spray or roll on 2 coats of Flat Water Base Exterior House.

MISCELLANEOUS

PROJECT: I want to paint my chain link fence and make it look like new.

CONDITION: Fencing has grown dark.

MATERIALS NEEDED: Aluminum Paint.

SPECIAL EQUIPMENT NEEDED: Stiff Push Broom, Throw away Gloves, Fence Roller, your oldest clothes (you will probably be throwing these away too).

TIME REQUIRED: 1 day (you will remember).

PROCEDURE:

1. Talk to your across the fence neighbor about what you are going to do. You may want to both do this at the same time.

2. Trim grass under and around fence low. Trim shrubs, etc., back.

3. Brush fence with a stiff garage broom. Clean away all the spider webs, etc.

4. Aluminum Paint is not mixed and you can not get it mixed at the store. The best way is to box all the Aluminum Paint.

   Boxing means pouring the paint back and forth between the containers until each gallon of paint is thoroughly mixed. After all the paint is thoroughly mixed, combine it in a 5 or 10 gallon bucket to make certain the paint color is uniform.

   When it is all mixed to a homogenized consistency, no yucky stuff on the bottom, pour a gallon into a 10 quart bucket. Pour the rest of the Aluminum Paint back into their respective pails and seal them.

   Now, Install a roller grid on the top of the bucket.

5. Put on your gloves and start rolling. Try not to paint the rose bushes aluminum. Get ready to apologize to the neighbor for ruining his prize what ever.

6. One coat and you're done for the next five to ten years. Unless you plan on going somewhere disguised as the Tin Man, take my advice and throw everything away: Roller, Bucket, Gloves, probably your clothes and shoes, too.

MISCELLANEOUS

PROJECT: My Aluminum Awnings are very discolored. I want to repaint them with a new color.

CONDITION: Discolored.

MATERIALS NEEDED: TSP, Water Base Stain Kill, Exterior Acrylic Water Base Trim Paint.

SPECIAL EQUIPMENT NEEDED: None.

TIME REQUIRED: 1 Day.

PROCEDURE:

1. If possible, take down awnings so that you do not have to do this on a ladder.

2. Clean with a solution of 3 or 4 oz. TSP to a gallon of water. Rinse with Garden hose. Remember that there is an outside and an under side. Do both.

3. Let dry 3 or 4 hours.

4. Apply a Water Base Stain Kill.

5. Let dry 4 hours.

MISCELLANEOUS

6. Paint with two coats of Exterior Acrylic Water Base Trim Paint. Do not paint early in the morning when dew is still on the awnings. The droplets of water in dew and fog can cause Dew Burn. The droplets stay on the surface and act like magnifying glasses, burning the newly applied, fragile paint.

7. Be sure to wait one day between coats.

PROJECT: I want to paint my cement porch to match the exterior trim.

Do not paint cement unless you did something very bad in a former life and want to spend the rest of your life repainting to make up for it. Actually, there are high performance cement coatings available, Imron® by DuPont High Performance Coatings and Final Finish™ by the Coronado Paint® Company specifically for this type of project. Bear in mind, they are premium products, at premium prices, that are only now being made available to the D.I.Y. market. If you want to go top of the line, look for them at your professional paint stores.

If your cement porch is not the most important part of your house, you will be better off staining, not painting the porch. Final Finish™ is classified by its makers as a stain. They would probably also classify the Star Ship Enterprise as an airplane.

MISCELLANEOUS

CONDITION: Good condition.

MATERIALS NEEDED: 20° Muratic Acid, Cement Stain.

SPECIAL EQUIPMENT NEEDED: Stiff Garage Brush, Long Handled Roller, Dual Canister Respirator.

TIME REQUIRED: 3 days.

PROCEDURE:

1. Clean and etch the cement with a solution of one part 20° Muratic Acid to three parts of water.

   Take proper precautions. Wear goggles, cuffed rubber gloves, a dual canister respirator, old long sleeved shirt, slacks, and shoes.

2. Rinse copiously.

3. Let dry one or 24 hours.

4. Apply one coat of a good Cement Stain. Apply with a roller with extension handle. If your heart is really set on cement paint and think that Final Finish™ and Imron® products are a little pricey, the Porter Paint Co. has come out with a cement product that is very good.

MISCELLANEOUS

PROJECT: I want to paint my new, hand made/ home made wood furniture.

CONDITION: Beautiful and new.

MATERIALS NEEDED: 120 Grit Sandpaper, TSP or Organic Cleaner, Water Base Wood Primer, Acrylic Exterior House or Exterior Trim Paint.

SPECIAL EQUIPMENT NEEDED: None.

TIME REQUIRED: 1-2 days.

PROCEDURE:

1. I know it's clean, but first, run your hand along the furniture and make certain there are not any rough edges that could snag a lady's hose or skirt. If there is even a hint, smooth out with some 120 Grit Sandpaper.

2. Wash with a solution of 2 oz. (dry measure) TSP per gallon of water, or a 5 to 1 Organic Cleaner solution. Rinse thoroughly.

3. Let dry 1 - 2 hours.

4. Turn the piece of furniture upside down. Now, brush on one coat of Water Base Wood Primer. Begin with the bottom of the chair legs/ table legs.

5. Let dry 4 hours minimum.

6. Turn the chair right side up. Paint on one coat of Latex Wood Primer. Begin with the top edges. If there are slats in the seat or back, make certain you cover the sides of the slats.

7. Let dry 4 hours minimum.

8. Now is the time to apply your finish coat. Seriously consider if you would not be just as happy with an Exterior Solid Wood Stain. The colors can be quite nice. The decision rests with the formality of your lawn setting. Stains are more rustic. Semi Gloss Trim Paint, a little more formal.

Let's get to work. Turn upside down again. Brush on 2 coats of your favorite Acrylic Water Base House or Trim Paint. You are going to have to do the bottoms and the tops, and the sides, just like the Primer.

Protecting the bottoms of the legs is extremely important. Moisture is often drawn up through the legs. The seat bottoms are always the last to dry and always absorb water.

MISCELLANEOUS

PROJECT: Oops! I didn't repaint my wood lawn furniture soon enough. The paint's flaking and I've got a little wood rot. How do I make it look beautiful and new.

CONDITION: Flaking Paint, Wood Rot.

MATERIALS NEEDED: TSP or Organic Cleaner, Exterior Wood Filler, 80 Grit Sandpaper, Exterior Oil Base Stain Kill, your choice of Oil Base or Water Base Finish Paint.

SPECIAL EQUIPMENT NEEDED: None.

TIME REQUIRED: 2 Days.

PROCEDURE:

1. Scrape and sand away loose flaking wood. Wire brush if necessary.

2. Wash with a 2 oz. TSP Solution, or a 5 to 1 Organic Cleaner Solution. Rinse thoroughly.

3. Let dry 4 - 6 hours.

4. Gouge out small areas of wood rot and replace with an Exterior Wood Filler. Fill in and smooth out. Let dry.

5. If you want to make certain that the surfaces are completely smooth, fill in any deep indentations caused by flaked off paint, with the Exterior Wood Filler. Sand smooth.

MISCELLANEOUS

6. Brush on one coat of an Oil Base Exterior Stain Kill. Please read and follow the painting sequence recommended in the previous tip. Bottom edges first, then tops and sides.

7. Let dry a minimum of 4 hours.

8. Apply two coats of your choice of an Oil or Water Base Semi Gloss Exterior House or Exterior Trim Paint. Make certain that the first coat is thoroughly dry before applying the second coat.

PROJECT: I want to give my new, unfinished wood lawn furniture a natural, varnished look.

CONDITION: New, raw wood.

MATERIALS NEEDED: Mineral Spirits, Marine Sealer and Marine Finish.

SPECIAL EQUIPMENT NEEDED: 150 Grit Sandpaper, Tack Rag.

TIME REQUIRED: 2 - 3 Days.

MISCELLANEOUS

PROCEDURE:

1. Check for rough spots with your bare hand. Sand any rough spots you find until the surface is smooth.

2. Wash the entire piece of furniture, top, bottom, sides, everything, with Mineral Spirits.

3. Let dry 1 hour.

4. Turn furniture upside down. Apply a liberal coat of Marine Sealer to the entire bottom surface. Be sure to get into all the nooks and crannies.

5. Right the piece and Tack Rag the top, sides, etc.

6. Apply the Sealer all over.

7. Let dry about 6 hours.

8. When dry, apply the Marine Finish to the back, arms and seat area only.

9. Apply second Marine Finish Coat. Important: do not wait more than 24 hours for the second coat.

MISCELLANEOUS

PROJECT: My varnished lawn furniture has yellowed and flaked in spots. I want to restore the beautiful, natural wood look.

CONDITION: Varnished yellow, flaking in some spots. Some wood rot.

MATERIALS NEEDED: 80 and 150 Grit Sandpaper, Household Chlorine Bleach, High Performance Wood Patch, Marine Sealer, Marine Finish.

SPECIAL EQUIPMENT NEEDED: Random Orbit Mechanical Sander.

TIME REQUIRED: 2 - 3 Days.

PROCEDURE:

1. Using the Random Orbit Mechanical Sander and 80 Grit Sandpaper, remove all the old finish.

2. Dust off.

3. Apply household Chlorine Bleach full strength to the entire wood surface. Swab it on. Do not let it dry. When wood has lightened, stop the chemical reaction by swabbing down with plain water.

4. Let dry.

5. Gouge out any rotted areas.

MISCELLANEOUS

6. Fill with High Performance Exterior Wood Patch.

7. The wood grain has raised from the Bleach and Water, sand smooth with 150 Grit Sandpaper.

8. Turn piece upside down. Dust off using a Tack Rag.

9. Apply the Marine Sealer to every nook and cranny.

10. Right the piece and Tack Rag the top, sides, etc.

11. Apply the Marine Sealer all over.

12. Let dry about 8 hours.

13. When dry, apply the Marine Finish to the back, arms and seat area only.

14. Apply second Marine Finish Coat. Important: do not wait more than 24 hours for the second coat.

MISCELLANEOUS

PROJECT: I want to paint exterior Wicker Furniture.

CONDITION: Good condition. Paint has worn away and flaking in spots. Original paint was on raw, untreated rattan.

MATERIALS NEEDED: TSP, Household Chlorine Bleach, Shellac Base Stain Kill Spray, Oil Base Enamel Paint.

SPECIAL EQUIPMENT NEEDED: None.

TIME REQUIRED: 3 days.

PROCEDURE:

1. Sand away flaking paint.

2. Wash with 4 oz. solution of TSP. If there has been a mold or mildew problem, add 1 cup Bleach to the Cleaning solution. Rinse thoroughly with a garden hose.

3. Spray on Shellac Base Stain Kill.

4. Let dry 2 hours.

5. Spray two coats of Oil Base Enamel Paint.

6. Store Wicker Furniture indoors during the winter if possible. If it must winter outside, raise above the ground. Cover with Tyvek™. Unlike ordinary plastic, Tyvek breaths and will permit the furniture to acclimatize to the change in seasons.

MISCELLANEOUS

After letting the paint cure about 3 weeks, apply a car paint sealant that includes Teflon, such as Diamond Brite™ or Finish 2001™ that contains Urethane.

Alternative

PROJECT: The paint on my old rattan furniture is wearing off. I want to repaint the wicker, without injuring the attached upholstered fabric.

CONDITION: Quality, wicker furniture. Some paint wearing down to the bear surface.

MATERIALS NEEDED: Blue Masking Tape, Plastic Wrap, PBC Deglosser or Liquid Sandpaper, Shellac Base Stain Kill in a spray can; Polyurethane Resin Spray Paint in a spray can.

SPECIAL EQUIPMENT NEEDED: None.

TIME REQUIRED: 1 Day.

PROCEDURE:

This should be done outside.

MISCELLANEOUS

1. If upholstery fabric, or plastic can not be taken off the rattan furniture easily, It should be carefully wrapped with Blue Masking Tape and plastic, for maximum protection.

2. Wash entire piece of furniture, 2 or 3 times, with Liquid Sandpaper, or PBC Deglosser. This is no time to be daydreaming You have to clean every millimeter of this furniture thoroughly.

3. Spray Furniture with one coat of Shellac Base Stain Kill Spray.

4. Let dry 1 or 2 hours.

5. Spray on 3 or 4 fine, light coats of a Polyurethane Spray Paint in your favorite color. This paint has almost no film build. It is therefore absolutely essential that you put on the recommended number of coats.

    Follow the directions on the spray can exactly. Shake very well. Shake often. Keep the spray can at least 18 inches away from the surface. Move can back and forth. Never hold can stationary or paint will begin to run.

MISCELLANEOUS

PROJECT: My varnished Rattan Furniture (Wicker) is beginning to wear. I want to refinish, but keep the same, natural look. No paint.

CONDITION: Furniture is in good condition. Varnish is beginning to wear through to the bare rattan. Major yellowing from age. Some flaking.

MATERIALS NEEDED: Paint & Varnish Remover in a Spray Can; BIX™ Stain Brush, Stain in a Spray Can, Spar Varnish or Polyurethane in a Spray Can.

SPECIAL EQUIPMENT NEEDED: None.

TIME REQUIRED: 1 1/2 Days.

PROCEDURE:

Do this outside if at all possible. Do not even think of doing this on a humid day (above 75%).

1. Spray a liberal coat of Paint and Varnish Remover on the piece of furniture. Follow can directions to the letter.

2. Scrape off with a wooden spatula or a #3 Steel Wool Pad.

3. Remove material from cracks and crevices with a BIX™ Stain Brush.

MISCELLANEOUS

4. Wash down furniture with Denatured Alcohol.

5. Inspect furniture minutely. If the faintest trace of old stain and varnish exists, redo the area, following steps 1 - 4.

   It is very important that every trace of the old finish be gone before you begin with the new. If it is not completely gone, the new finish will not adhere to the old, and you will have a splotchy looking job.

6. Spray on one coat of stain in your choice of finishes.

7. Reinspect the entire piece of furniture to make certain that all of the old finish has been removed. Old particles should be more obvious after the furniture has been stained.

8. Spray on 3 to 4 coats of a Spray Varnish. Use a Spar Varnish or an Exterior Polyurethane.

   Spray on very light coats of varnish, just like you were painting. Follow can directions to the letter. Pay particular attentions to "Tack Free" time. Do not, under any conditions, spray a subsequent coat, until the "Tack Free Time Period" has elapsed. At the same time, do not wait much longer than the recommended interval between coats.

MISCELLANEOUS

PROJECT: I want to paint my steel or wrought iron furniture.

CONDITION: Weathered and rusty.

MATERIALS NEEDED: TSP, Good Anti-Rust Primer and Metal Paint or Hammerite Metal Finish Paint.

SPECIAL EQUIPMENT NEEDED: 3/8" Power Drill and Wire Wheel or Wire Brush.

TIME REQUIRED: 1 Day.

PROCEDURE:

1. Brush off loose rust with a 3/8" Power Drill and Wire Wheel or Wire Brush.

2. Clean metal furniture with a solution of 3 oz. TSP per gallon of water. Rinse with garden hose.

3. Let dry completely, at least two hours.

4. You can paint with a metal anti-rust primer and then recoat with good metal paint.

   If you prefer, you can use a Hammerite Metal Finish™. This product can be sprayed directly over rusted areas because it bonds to even rusted metal and seals it. One good coat is all that is necessary.

MISCELLANEOUS

PROJECT: I want to change the color of my white plastic Lawn Furniture.

CONDITION: A little worn and dirty.

MATERIALS NEEDED: Easy Surface Prep by the Flood Company, Water Base Stain Kill, Oil Base Exterior Enamel (Floor Paint works Great).

SPECIAL EQUIPMENT NEEDED: None.

TIME REQUIRED: 1 Day.

PROCEDURE:

1. Wipe surface with Easy Surface Prep.

2. Let dry.

3. Apply one coat of Water Base Stain Kill.

4. Let dry.

5. Finish with two coats of Oil Base Exterior Enamel. Both coats must be applied within a 24 hour period or the paint will not cure properly.

6. Enjoy. You're done.

MISCELLANEOUS

PROJECT: I want to treat my new Cedar Picnic Table. I want it to retain its natural color, but have a high gloss, "furniture finish."

CONDITION: Beautiful but untreated.

MATERIALS NEEDED: Mineral Spirits, Sikken's Cetol™.

SPECIAL EQUIPMENT NEEDED: None.

TIME REQUIRED: Check can instructions.

PROCEDURE:

1. Wash down with Mineral Spirits.

2. Let dry.

3. Apply three coats of Sikkens to the entire table. Underside, legs, everything. Make certain that the entire piece is encapsulated, bottoms, sides, edges, everything.

MISCELLANEOUS

PROJECT: I want to re-varnish my Cedar Picnic Table. It is beginning to yellow. I want to bring back its natural beauty, color, and finish.

CONDITION: Some yellowing and dry rot.

MATERIALS NEEDED: Mineral Spirits, Household Chlorine Bleach, 80 and 150 Grit Sandpaper, Tack Rag, Marine Sealer and Marine Finish Coat.

SPECIAL EQUIPMENT NEEDED: Random Orbit Sander.

TIME REQUIRED: 3 days.

PROCEDURE:

1. Sand off all the old finish with the Random Orbit Sander and 80 Grit Sandpaper.

2. Wash with Mineral Spirits.

3. If dark areas are evident, apply household Chlorine Bleach to the entire table. Do not let dry. When the dark spots have been bleached, stop the chemical action with large amounts of clean water.

MISCELLANEOUS

4. Let dry at least 2 hours.

5. Sand smooth and quiet the grain with 150 Grit Sandpaper.

6. Dust off then Tack Rag.

7. Turn upside down and coat entire bottom surface with 1 coat of Marine Sealer.

8. Turn right side up and apply 1 coat of Marine Sealer to the entire surface, edges, etc.

9. Let dry.

10. Apply two coats of Marine Finish to the Eating and Seating areas.

MISCELLANEOUS

PROJECT: I want to treat my children's new cedar play set to keep it looking natural. (Same tip for Rough Cedar Lawn Furniture.)

CONDITION: Newly Constructed.

MATERIALS NEEDED: Wood Toner/Sealer.

SPECIAL EQUIPMENT NEEDED: None.

TIME REQUIRED: One full, clear day.

PROCEDURE:

1. My suggestion is to not use a sealer that contains Hydrocarbons. Apply a Penofin or CWF UV Sealer.

2. Try to keep the kids off until it dries.

3. Enjoy.

MISCELLANEOUS

PROJECT: My Children's Varnished Cedar Swing Set is getting yellowed. I want to refinish it to bring back its natural beauty.
(Same tip for rough sawn cedar lawn furniture)

CONDITION: Yellowed and peeling.

MATERIALS NEEDED: Paint & Varnish Remover, Mineral Spirits, Marine Sealer and Marine Finish.

SPECIAL EQUIPMENT NEEDED: None.

TIME REQUIRED: 3 days.

PROCEDURE:

1. Remove all the old finish with a heavy bodied Paint and Varnish Remover.

2. Wash down with Mineral Spirits.

3. Let dry.

4. Refinish with one coat of Marine Sealer.

5. Apply two coats of Marine Finish.

MISCELLANEOUS

PROJECT: I want to treat my children's pressure treated swing set.

CONDITION: New.

MATERIALS NEEDED: Mineral Spirits, Seasonite™.

SPECIAL EQUIPMENT NEEDED: None.

TIME REQUIRED: 1 Day.

PROCEDURE:

1. Wash set down with Mineral Spirits.

2. Let dry about 1 hour.

3. Apply a liberal coat of Seasonite to the entire surface. Make certain you cover all edges and grain.

4. You're done.

5. In two or three years, apply a pigmented Exterior Stain.

MISCELLANEOUS

PROJECT: I have a metal bench with varnished wood slats. Both need refinishing.

CONDITION: Rusting metal; yellowing varnish.

MATERIALS NEEDED: Metal Frame: Liquid Deglosser, Hammerite™ Paint. Wood Slats: Sandpaper, Deck Brightener, Spar or Marine Varnish.

SPECIAL EQUIPMENT NEEDED: Dual Cartridge Respirator.

TIME REQUIRED: 2 days.

PROCEDURE:

Do wood portion first. Make certain you are working outside.

Slats:

Remember a wood slat has six sides. Treat all six sides.

1. Powder Sand with 120 grit garnet Sandpaper.

2. Wash with an Oxalic Acid based deck brightener.

MISCELLANEOUS

Follow directions to the letter. Be sure to wear goggles, rubber gloves, dual cartridge respirator, long sleeved shirt, slacks and shoes.

3. Dry one day.

4. Apply three coats of spar or helm varnish.

Metal Frame:

1. Wash with Liquid Deglosser.

2. Let Dry.

3. Repaint with Hammerite in the color of your choice. Two coats.

Alternate:

1. Apply one coat of Extend™ to rusty metal only.

2. Let cure.

3. Apply 2 coats of Rustoleum Enamel.

4. You're done! (And so am I. Happy memories.)

Painting the great outdoors

WHEN IT COMES TO EXTERIOR PAINTING, most people think only of their house. But, according to experts at the Rohm and Haas Paint Quality Institute, there are many other outside surfaces around your home that can be beautified and protected with top quality acrylic latex paint. Pictured above are just a few: gutters and downspouts, fencing, your children's swing set, the dog house, and the family picnic table. If you have some paint left over, put it to good use on other items, such as the utility shed, lightposts, mailboxes, outdoor furniture, and metal doors and windows. Painting these areas can add an attractive splash of color to your house and yard.

GLOSSARY

GLOSSARY

Acrylic: A synthetic polymer binder used in Latex Paints. Improves paint life and color retention. One of the signs of a premium quality paint.

Adhesion: Paint's ability to hold to surface without peeling, flaking or blistering.

Airless Sprayer: Spray equipment that uses hydraulic pressure, instead of air pressure, to atomize paint.

Alkyd Oil Based Paint: Oil based paint made from synthetic resins. Used for both interior, exterior and metal coatings. One of the signs of a premium quality paint.

Alligatoring: Paint failure with cracks appearing in a rectangular pattern.

Anti-Rust Primer: Primer with rust inhibitor additive.

Atomize: Breaking up of paint or other substance into tiny droplets.

Back Priming: Priming of the back side of exterior wood that will not be visible after installation.

Base Coat: Undercoat of paint upon which other paints are applied.

Binder: One of three main ingredients of paint. Determines paint's performance properties: washability, toughness, adhesion, durability and fade resistance.

Bleaching: Fading of color due to ultra violet rays of the sun. Also, the use of Oxalic Acid or other bleaching agent to lighten or restore natural wood color.

GLOSSARY

Bleeding: Reappearance of old paint color or stain through new coat, necessitating use of stain kill before final coat.

Blistering: Formation of air pockets in paint caused by heat or moisture.

Boxing: Mixing of gallons of the same color paint in a larger container to assure even color throughout the job.

Bridging: The filling of surface cracks, voids and pores by paint.

Build Up: The accumulated thickness of coats of paint on a surface.

Casement Window: Window that opens outward like a door.

Caulking: Flexible filler for holes, joints and trim. Seals out cold and moisture; also fills gaps to provide a solid appearance.

Chalking: Gradual disintegration of paint surface into a powdery substance.

Checking: Small, vertical cracks in paint.

Color Retention: Ability of paint to resist fading.

Consistency: Density of paint.

Cracking: Breaks in paint surface.

Custom Mixed Paint: Paint mixed at store to specific color selection, usually from swatches.

GLOSSARY

Cutting-In: Use of a small brush or roller to provide constant paint coverage around doors and windows, at corners, and the junction of wall and ceiling.

Deglosser: Chemical agent that takes the high sheen off of painted surface to make new coat of paint adhere better.

Deglossing: Taking the shine off glossy surfaces, such as enamel, by roughening with sandpaper or chemicals to make adhesion better for a new coat of paint.

Double Hung Windows: Vertically opening windows.

Drop Cloth: A large piece of canvas, plastic or paper designed to protect floors, furniture, and other objects from accidental splashing during paint application.

Dry Measure: Measurement of ingredients in dry not liquid form.

Dry to Recoat: Paint dry enough for next application.

Dry to Touch: Paint has dried sufficiently so that a light touch will not make finger marks.

Durability: Degree to which paint resists weathering from sun, rain, wind, heat, cold, etc.

Eggshell Paint: Low luster paint finish.

Elasticity: Ability of paint to expand and contract from heat and cold without changing appearance, cracking or losing adhesion.

GLOSSARY

Enamel: Typically a paint that dries to a hard, smooth finish. Comes in both Latex and Oil Based Satin, Flat, Semi Gloss, and High Gloss varieties. Made for both interior and exterior use.

Epoxy: A resin based paint used on non-porous surfaces. Very hard and durable, it dries by chemical action, no evaporation. Special care and training is needed to use this paint successfully.

Extender: A lower cost additive, like clay, that extends pigment's capabilities and/or adds bulk to paint by adding density to paints consistency.

Extension Handle: Four to six foot handle that attaches to rollers and sanding pads , for use on painting and prepping walls and ceilings.

Fading: Lightening of color due to sun.

Ferrule: The metal band that goes around a paint brush and holds the bristles in place.

Fillers: Products used to fill in cracks or holes in wood, plaster, dry wall or masonry.

Film Build: Progressive recoating to provide surface protection.

Film Thickness: Depth of coating in mils.

Fire Retardant Paint: Latex paints with heat resistant properties caused by the addition of silicone or other fire resistant chemicals.

GLOSSARY

Film Formation: Paint's ability to form a solid film after the evaporation of the thinner.

Finish Coat: The top coat of paint.

Flaking: Breaking away of small pieces of paint from the substrate caused by failure of paint's adhesion characteristics.

Flat Paint: A luster free paint made for both interior and exterior use.

Gloss: The reflectivity of paint. High gloss paint reflects light and highlights surface irregularities. Flat gloss paints have low reflectivity.

Grain: The natural pattern of wood.

Hiding Power: Ability of paint to cover original surface color. Provided by pigment.

Knot: A part of the pattern of the wood. It marks the place where a branch was growing. May have to be sealed before painting or varnishing.

Latex Paint: Water based paint made with synthetic binders. Soap and water cleanup.

Laying Off: With paint it means the uniform direction of the finish stroke. With varnish, it can mean the final stroke, plus the cross stroke sometimes needed at the edge of the surface to prevent running.

Laying On Paint: The act of bringing the supply of paint or varnish from the can to the surface. Not a finishing stroke.

GLOSSARY

Leveling: Ability of paint to form a smooth coat with no brush marks.

Liquid Sandpaper: Chemical deglossing agent painted on hard or glossy surface to make paint adhere.

Masonry: Poured or block concrete, bricks or stone.

Masonry Paint: Special Oil or Latex Paints especially designed for use on masonry surfaces.

Masking: Covering of an area to protect it from accidental paint coverage.

Masking Tape: Paper tape used to protect non-painted surfaces from accidental painting. New grades leave no adhesive residue, when left for long periods of time.

Mildew: A living fungus that thrives on paint proteins and high moisture environments.

Mildewcide: Chemical agent that inhibits growth of mildew when added to paints.

Mineral Spirits: Solvent that has been distilled from petroleum.

Muriatic Acid: Commercial hydrochloric acid used to clean alkali deposits from masonry.

Mullion: Wood, plaster or metal divider between window panes.

Oil Base Paint: Paint made with linseed or other vegetable oils. Cleans and thins with paint thinner or mineral spirits.

GLOSSARY

Orbital Sander: Machine sander with a rectangular pressure pad.

Paint: Oil or water based coating made from a combination of solvents, pigments and resins.

Paint Thinner: Water, mineral spirits, or turpentine used to clean or thin paint.

Paint Tray: Paint container for use with roller.

Patching Compound: Plaster or vinyl paste used to fill holes and cracks in wood, plaster or drywall before painting.

Peeling: Ribbons of paint formed by paint's loss of adhesion characteristics.

Penetrating Oils: Tunge, Linseed, or Rosewood Oils used to waterproof, seal or finish wood.

Pigment: One of paint's three basic components.   The finely ground particles that provide paint's color and opacity.

Polymer: In paint, a substance consisting of giant molecules formed from smaller petrochemical molecules to improve paint's binding characteristics.

Polyurethane: A very durable clear varnish used for floors, countertops and trim.

Porosity: Absorption quality of wood, masonry, etc.

Primer: Oil, or Latex base coat that penetrates and seals surface to be painted.

GLOSSARY

Quiet the grain: Light sanding of wood grain caused by reaction to chemical treatment of wood.

Retarder: A colorless gel mixed with some water-based paints to retard drying time by slowing evaporation.

Resins: Chief binding agent in paints. Synthetically produced resins are used in alkyds, acrylics and urethanes.

Roller: Cylinder shaped paint applicator formed by filling a roller cover over a roller frame.

Roller Cover: Sleeve over roller frame that provides the actual applicator.

Sash Brush: Angled or straight bristle brush especially designed for painting window sashes and moldings.

Satin Finish Paint: A paint finish that has a slightly higher sheen rate than eggshell. It is about midway between gloss and flat paint.

Scaffolding: A platform supported by a metal frame, for painting or other wall or ceiling work.

Scraper: A metal tool used to remove paint.

Sealer: A clear coat product which penetrates wood or masonry and serves as a barrier to moisture and dirt. This is essential protection for decks and concrete driveways.

Sheen: The reflective quality of paint. Often expressed as a "high" sheen rate for high gloss enamels, and a "low" sheen rate for flat paints.

GLOSSARY

Shellac: The same word is used for both the resin and the thin, clear varnish made from a mixture of this resin and alcohol.

Siding: The wood, metal or vinyl covering that provides the exterior surface of a house.

Skin: Drying paint slick that forms over the surface of oil base paint.

Sleeve: Roller cover.

Solvents: Paint thinners, such as water or mineral spirits. One of three main ingredients in paint.

Spalling: Deterioration of unsealed, water logged, brick and cement. It is caused by the freezing and expansion of the absorbed water, breaking off large chips of the brick or cement surface.

Spar Varnish: Oil based exterior varnish.

Spattering: Droplets of paint that spin off when roller is used.

Stain: Coloring and protective coating used on wood or cement. Soaks in, does not lay on top like paint. Important: Cement stain and wood stain are two different products. They are not interchangeable.

Stain: Also mean the accidental discoloring of a surface area by paint, scorching, mildew, etc.

GLOSSARY

Stain Blocker: Coating applied to old or discolored surface to prevent color from bleeding through new paint.

Steel Wool: Available in many grades and used for final preparation of painted or varnished surface. Area must be tack ragged carefully before painting to assure that all filaments have been removed.

Stripper: Heat based, or chemical agent used to strip paint from wood and metal surfaces.

Tack Rag: Sticky cloth used to clean final dust, sawdust, steel wool residue from surface before painting or varnishing a surface.

Tacky Surface: Slightly sticky newly painted surface caused by improper drying.

Thinner: One of three major ingredients to paint. In Oil Based Paints this is a turpentine or linseed oil. In Latex Paints, this is water.

Thixotropic Paint: Non-drip Alkyd, Oil Based Paint.

Tipping Off: Touching off the tips of the bristles of a brush to the sides of the paint can to make certain that there is not too much paint or varnish in the brush.

Trim: Decorative wood, vinyl or metal applied to surface to improve aesthetic effect.

Trim Paint: Hard enamel paint applied to trim surfaces.

TSP: Trisodium Phosphate. A strong cleaning agent used to clean and degrease surfaces before painting. In stronger

GLOSSARY

solutions it can actually degloss paint. New, environmentally benign formulations of TSP are now available for use in States which restrict Phosphate use.

Tung Oil: Oil of Tung tree used in fine wood finishing paints.

Turpentine: Paint thinner made from the sap of the pine tree. Can replace mineral spirits. Although it has a pungent odor, it does not have toxic fumes.

Ultra Violet Rays: Destructive rays from the sun that prematurely discolor and age wood (Imagine what it does to human skin).

Undercoat: A layer of paint applied before the final coat of paint. This is usually applied to provide a smooth, stain free surface.

UV: Abbreviation for Ultra Violet.

UV Blocker: The ingredient in a sealer, stain or paint that impedes penetration of destructive Ultra Violet Rays.

UV Coating: A coating designed to impede the penetration of Ultra Violet Rays. For exterior use. Used primarily on decks and siding.

Urethane: A durable, clear varnish. The same as polyurethane.

Varnish: A clear, usually high gloss, or semi gloss, oil based finish coat used on wood surfaces. Provides luster and protection while permitting the natural beauty of the wood grain to show.

GLOSSARY

Vehicle: Combination of binder and thinner that, when combined with pigment, creates paint.

Vinyl: A synthetic resin most often used in Latex Paint. Polyvinyl Chloride (PVC) is sometimes used in Oil Based Paint where high chemical resistance is necessary.

Viscosity: The resistance to spread or flow of paint.

V.O.C.: Volatile Organic Content. Technically any carbon compound that evaporates under standard test conditions. For our purposes, any paint solvent except water that evaporates. V.O.C. may be a concern to air purity standards.

V.O.C. Paints: Paints that conform to higher air quality standards.

V.O.C. Stains: Stains that conform to higher air quality standards.

V.O.C. Varnishes: Varnishes that conform to higher air quality standards. These varnishes have a very low "build rate" and multiple coats are always necessary.

Volume Solids: The volume of Pigment and Binder solids expressed as a percent. The thicker the paint, the larger the percentage of Binder and Pigment by volume.

Washability: Ability to remove dirt from paint surface without causing damage to paint.

Water Repellent: The silicone or acrylic powder used to make special "waterproof" paint for wood.

GLOSSARY

Wood Graining: Creation of a wood grain look on any surface using a combination of base coat, stain coats, and special brushes and squeegees, plus a final protective polyurethane coat.

Wood Preservatives: Toxic liquids painted on, or impregnated into wood under high pressure, to protect against insects, fungi, and rotting.

Wood Putty: A hard drying, relatively strong material used to patch holes in wood prior to painting. May be sanded, drilled, painted, or stained like the wood that surrounds it.

Wrinkling: Wrinkled paint failure caused by improper paint application. Paint was applied too thickly and the top coat dried before the bottom coat.

INDEX

INDEX

INDEX

INDEX

INDEX

INDEX

Ask your retailer about more of Glenn Haege's books.

If your store is out of stock, turn page for Direct Order Information.

FIX IT
FAST & EASY!

By
Glenn Haege

America's Master Handyman Answers the Most Asked "How To" Questions.

"A treasure trove of answers to the most asked 'How To' questions....the book tells the easiest way to do many of the hardest cleaning and fix-up chores."
Kathleen Kavaney Zuleger
Book Review

"From handling mildew problems to revitalizing a deck and sprucing up furniture, this book has hints others miss; such as the peculiarities of renewing a redwood deck, and getting rid of mold in a stored refrigerator. It is these tips on common yet seldom-addressed problems which make this such an important home reference."
The Bookwatch

"Each problemish project is tackled head-on, staged in steps, and provided with all essential information like what to use to get the desired result."
Marilis Hornidge *Book bag*

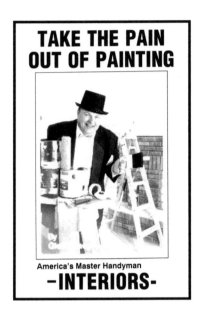

TAKE THE PAIN OUT OF PAINTING

America's Master Handyman

-INTERIORS-

"Finally: a guide to interior do-it-yourself painting which follows a very simple yet information-packed step-by-step format!"

"Haege's includes extensive details on stain kills, rating paints by their stain-resistant abilities as well as special application and finish requirements. A very basic, essential home reference"

The Bookwatch

"Haege has consolidated his years of painting knowledge....he gives save-facingly simple step-by-step answers on how to solve them."

Albany Herald

"the first how-to manual to demistify the arcane world of stain kills ...Haege makes it easy for anyone smart enough to lift a paint can lid...to solve a particualar painting problem."

The Detroit News

Glenn Haege's COMPLETE DECK CARE GUIDE 2⁹⁵

Everything You Need to Know to Keep Your Deck Looking Its Best

Takes all the confusion out of deck care! Gives simple, easy to follow directions on how to keep your deck looking great.

Glenn Haege's COMPLETE DECK CARE GUIDE **cuts through all the advertising claims. It is the Do-It-Yourselfer's only complete, unbiased source of answers to these questions:**

How do you bring back the original beauty to a graying deck?

What should you put on your deck?

What's the difference between Wood Sealers, Toners, UV Coatings, Wood Stains?

What's the best way to service your deck and how often do you need to do it?

TO: Glenn Haege
Master Handyman Press, Inc.
P.O. Box 1498
Royal Oak, MI. 48068-1498

Please send me copies of the following books:
All books are sold with a 100% money back, satisfaction guaranty:

_____	**FIX IT FAST & EASY!**	**@ $14.95 each**
_____	**TAKE THE PAIN OUT OF PAINTING!**	
_____	**- INTERIORS -**	**@ $17.95 each**
_____	**TAKE THE PAIN OUT OF PAINTING!**	
_____	**-EXTERIORS-**	**@ $12.95 each**
_____	**Glenn Haege's COMPLETE DECK**	
_____	**CARE GUIDE**	**@ $ 2.95 each**

Total $ _____

Michigan Residents: Please add 4% Sales Tax.

Shipping: $ 2 for the first book and $ 1 for each additional. If ordering only Glenn Haege's COMPLETE DECK CARE GUIDE, pay a shipping charge of $ 1 only.

FIRST BOOK AT $ 2.00: _____

ALL OTHER BOOKS AT $ 1.00: _____

TOTAL SHIPPING: _____

Total $ _____

Name: _____

Address: _____

_____ ZIP: _____

Please charge my _____ Visa _____ Master Card

Expiration Date: _____ Card # _____

Name on Card: _____

Signature: _____

Mail to:

Master Handyman Press, Inc.
P.O. Box 1498
Royal Oak, MI 48068-1498

or Call: 1-800-524-5391

TO: **Glenn Haege**
Master Handyman Press, Inc.
P.O. Box 1498
Royal Oak, MI. 48068-1498

(Photo copies of this form will not be honored for Free Book)

Please send me copies of the following books:
All books are sold with a 100% money back, satisfaction guaranty:

_____	**FIX IT FAST & EASY!**	**@ $14.95 each**
_____	**TAKE THE PAIN OUT OF PAINTING!**	
_____	**- INTERIORS -**	**@ $17.95 each**
_____	**TAKE THE PAIN OUT OF PAINTING!**	
_____	**-EXTERIORS-**	**@ $12.95 each**
_____	**Glenn Haege's COMPLETE DECK**	
_____	**CARE GUIDE**	**@ $ 2.95 each**

Total $ _____

Michigan Residents: Please add 4% Sales Tax.

Shipping: $ 2 for the first book and $ 1 for each additional. If ordering only Glenn Haege's COMPLETE DECK CARE GUIDE, fill out coupon on back and send in to get your free book.

FIRST BOOK AT $ 2.00: _____
ALL OTHER BOOKS AT $ 1.00: _____
TOTAL SHIPPING: _____

Total $ _____

Name: _____
Address: _____
_____ ZIP: _____

Please charge my _____ Visa _____ Master Card
Expiration Date:_____ Card # _____
Name on Card:_____
Signature:_____

CUT OUT THIS PAGE
FOR YOUR FREE COPY OF
Glenn Haege's **COMPLETE DECK CARE GUIDE**

SEND TO:
NAME: _____

Address: _____

CITY: _____ STATE:_____ ZIP:_____

Book Purchased from: _____

OFFER ENDS DECEMBER 31,1994

Mail to:

Master Handyman Press, Inc.
P.O. Box 1498
Royal Oak, MI 48068-1498

or Call: 1-800-524-5391